Step-by-Step Classic Kitchen

A hundred graded recipes with kitchen hints and wine guide

Wordsworth Editions

Step-by-Step Classic Kitchen

Fish

There is no finer food than that found in the seas, rivers and lakes of the world; it is natural, rich and above all, varied.

Fish have always been considered beneficial to health, being rich in animal protein as well as in phosphorous, iodine, sulphur, and various vitamins. They also contain the minimum of fat, even the so-called oily fish having less fat than lean meat.

This book is designed not only to help you in the preparation of a wide range of fish, but also to give you information about their habitat, how to choose the best fish, checking for freshness, the right fish for the right recipe and whether the fish should be well cooked, raw or marinated.

You may well be surprised at the variety of fish included. To many people, fish means cod or plaice, probably cooked in batter, but in fact there are dozens of kinds of edible fish. The fish stall in a large open market is a good place to see a really wide selection, including some of the more unusual fish mentioned in this book: a good stall may well have over 30 kinds of fish.

You may also be surprised at the number of ways there are of cooking fish. There are recipes here to suit all tastes, from raw marinated fish for the adventurous to classic dishes such as sole meunière or trout with almonds for elegant dinner parties, and hearty fish stews such as bouillabaisse when you have a lot of mouths to feed.

Whatever your tastes, we are sure you will enjoy this book. We hope it will give you inspiration, and encourage you to experiment with some of the more exotic and unusual fish.

Table of Contents

Each dish is followed by its total preparation and cooking time. (See note 1 on facing page.)

The star (★) system used throughout the book, indicating the degree of simplicity or difficulty of each recipe, is as follows:

★ *Very easy* ★ ★ *Easy* ★ ★ ★ *Difficult*

Shad
page
Shad with Sorrel *(1 hr 55 min)* ★ 6

Anchovy
Anchovies Tourtière *(50 min)* ★ 6
Gratin of Anchovies with Potatoes ★ ★ 8
(1 hr 20 min)
Gratin of Anchovies with Herbs *(50 min)* ★ ★ 8
Anchovies with Capers and Olives ★ ★ 8
(50 min)

Eel
Eels in Red Wine *(1 hr 10 min)* ★ ★ 9
Baked Eels *(40 min)* ★ 9
Eels with Spinach *(40 min)* ★ ★ 10
Eel Casserole *(40 min)* ★ ★ 10
Eel with Tomatoes *(55 min)* ★ ★ 12
Marinated and Grilled Eels *(25 min)* ★ ★ 12

Bass
Bass in White Wine *(50 min)* ★ ★ 13
Bass in Ginger *(50 min)* ★ ★ ★ 14

Brill
Brill with Rhubarb *(1 hr)* ★ ★ 13
Brill with Tomato and Cream *(45 min)* ★ ★ 14

Angler
Angler with Vegetables *(40 min)* ★ ★ 16
Angler with Milk and Cream *(30 min)* ★ 16
Angler Gratin with Cream *(45 min)* ★ 17
Tail of Angler with Pink Garlic *(40 min)* ★ 17

Pike
Pike with Cream and Walnuts *(25 min)* ★ 18
Sauté of Pike with Mushrooms *(30 min)* ★ ★ 18

Cod
Cod with Capers *(35 min)* ★ 20
Cod with Fresh Vegetables *(55 min)* ★ 20
Grilled Cod with Anchovy Butter ★ 21
(20 min)

Carp
Carp Jewish-Style *(1 hr)* ★ ★ ★ 21

Dorado
Dorado with Shellfish *(1 hr)* ★ 22
Dorado Tahiti-Style *(30 min)* ★ 22
Dorado with Salt *(55 min)* ★ 24
Dorado with Red Peppers *(1 hr 10 min)* ★ ★ 24
Fillets of Dorado with Lime *(1 hr)* ★ ★ ★ 25
Dorado with Herbs *(40 min)* ★ 25
Gratin of Dorado Venetian-Style ★ ★ 26
(45 min)
Dorado Bercy (baked with herbs) ★ 26
(45 min)

Dorado (continued)
page
Stewed Dorado with Herbs *(1 hr 5 min)* ★ ★ 28
Dorado with Capers *(1 hr)* ★ ★ 28

Haddock
Haddock in Milk *(20 min)* ★ 29
Haddock with Lemon *(25 min)* ★ 29

Herring
Herrings with Bacon *(35 min)* ★ ★ 30
Salted Herring with White Wine ★ ★ 30
(35 min)

Saithe
Stewed Saithe *(55 min)* ★ 32
Saithe with Olives *(55 min)* ★ ★ 32
Grilled Saithe with Caper Sauce *(10 min)* ★ 33

Dab
Dab with Prawns *(35 min)* ★ ★ 33
Dab with Cider *(35 min)* ★ ★ 34
Steamed Dab Fillets *(25 min)* ★ ★ 34

Mackerel
Marinated Mackerel with Cinnamon ★ 36
(30 min)
Mackerel in White Wine *(30 min)* ★ 36
Mackerel with Onions *(45 min)* ★ 37

Whiting
Stuffed Whiting *(35 min)* ★ ★ 37
Fried Whiting with Parsley *(20 min)* ★ 37
Whiting with White Wine *(35 min)* ★ ★ 38
Whiting with Fennel Seeds *(35 min)* ★ 38
Whiting with Spinach *(35 min)* ★ ★ 40
Stuffed Whiting with Mushrooms ★ ★ ★ 40
(1 hr)

Hake
Hake with Onions *(55 min)* ★ 41
Hake Gratin *(35 min)* ★ 41
Hake with Peppers *(55 min)* ★ ★ 42
Hake with Orange *(35 min)* ★ 42

Salt Cod
Salt Cod with Milk and Potatoes ★ 42
(45 min)
Salt Cod Balls with Basil *(1 hr)* ★ ★ 44
Salt Cod Gratin with Tomato Sauce ★ ★ 44
(1 hr)
Salted Cod Gratin with Onions *(45 min)* ★ ★ 45
Salt Cod Gratin with Milk *(50 min)* ★ ★ 45
Salt Cod Aioli *(50 min)* ★ ★ 46
Brandade of Salt Cod *(45 min)* ★ ★ 46
Salt Cod Gratin with Oregano ★ ★ 48
(1 hr 15 min)
Salt Cod with Currants *(45 min)* ★ 48

Mullet

		page
Roast Grey Mullet with Herbs (45 min)	★	49
Grey Mullet Provencal-Style (50 min)	★★	49
Grey Mullet with Herbs (35 min)	★	50
Grey Mullet with Cream and Peppers (50 min)	★	50

Perch

Perch Fillets with Sage (20 min)	★	52
Perch with Cream and Mushrooms (50 min)	★★	52

Skate

Skate with Black Butter (45 min)	★	53

Red Mullet

Red Mullet in Foil (30 min)	★	53
Red Mullet with Tomato Sauce (50 min)	★★	54
Red Mullet Oriental-Style (25 min)	★	54

Dogfish

Dogfish with Golden Rice (30 min)	★★	56
Dogfish with Saffron Sauce (1 hr)	★★	56

John Dory

John Dory with Leeks (45 min)	★★	57

Pike-Perch

Pike-Perch with Butter Sauce (30 min)	★★★	57

Sardines

Stuffed Sardines in the Oven (1 hr)	★★	58
Baked Sardines with Lemon Juice (30 min)	★	58
Sardines with Bay Leaves (45 min)	★	60
Chilled Sardines with Fennel (1 hr 15 min)	★★	60
Marinated Sardines with Onions (25 min)	★	61

Salmon

		page
Salmon with Sultanas (40 min)	★	61
Raw Salmon with Green Pepper (15 min)	★	62
One-Way Salmon (10 min)	★	62

Sole

Sole Fillets with Chives (20 min)	★★	64
Sole Fillets with Vermouth (25 min)	★★	64
Sole Meunière (10 min)	★	65
Sole in Seaweed (25 min)	★★	65
Fillets of Sole Fried with Lemon (15 min)	★	66
Sole Colbert (35 min)	★★	66
Sole Fillets with Cream (50 min)	★★★	68
Sole with Almonds and Herbs (35 min)	★★	68
Sole Fillets with Fresh Tagliatelle (30 min)	★★	69
Sole with Muscadet (35 min)	★★	69

Tuna

Sweet and Sour Tuna (35 min)	★★	70
Grilled Tuna with Herbs (20 min)	★	70
Tuna Italian-Style (30 min)	★	72

Trout

Trout with Butter and Wine (30 min)	★★	72
Trout with Almonds (25 min)	★★	73
Trout with Mustard and Cream (35 min)	★	73

Turbot

Turbot with Small Onions (1 hr)	★★	74
Chicken Turbot with Vegetables (1 hr)	★★	74

Mixed Fish Dishes

Mixed Grill of Marinated Fish (20 min)	★	76
Dieppe Fish-Pot (1 hr)	★★★	76
Bouillabaisse (55 min)	★★	77
Flemish Fish-Pot (1 hr)	★★★	77
Fish Soup with Tomatoes (55 min)	★★	78
Provençal Fish-Pot (1 hr 10 min)	★★★	78

Notes: Getting the Best out of this Book

1. The preparation times given in the Table of Contents and with each recipe are minimum times: they will vary according to the cook's ability and the equipment available. Certain of the recipes require periods for marinading or chilling. These have not been taken into account in the times given in the table, but are indicated at the head of each recipe.

2. It is best to use double cream for most recipes – it is the nearest equivalent to French cream. Remember also that the French use unsalted butter, and this is assumed in the recipes unless otherwise stated.

3. It is always best to use red or white wine vinegar in the recipes where vinegar is required; the results will not be the same if you use malt vinegar. In the same way, freshly ground black pepper should always be used in preference to ready-ground pepper.

4. Oven temperatures. The following are Gas, Fahrenheit and Centigrade equivalents:

Gas	¼	½	1	2	3	4	5	6	7	8	9
°F	225	250	275	300	325	350	375	400	425	450	475
°C	110	120	140	160	170	180	190	200	220	230	250

5. It is important when using these recipes to follow the exact proportions. A set of kitchen scales, measuring jug, glass and spoons are essential. Follow either metric *or* avoirdupois measurements in each recipe.

6. To help you choose the right wine for your meal, see page 80.

Alose à l'Oseille
Shad with Sorrel

Serves 4. Preparation: 20 min Cooking: 1 hr 35 min

★

- ○ **1.2kg (2½ lb) shad**
- ○ **500g (18 oz) fresh sorrel**
- ○ **1 slice raw ham**
- ○ **2 onions, finely chopped**
- ○ **30ml (2 tbls) oil**
- ○ **100ml (3½ fl oz) brandy**
- ○ **salt and pepper**

1. Scale, clean and wash the fish under cold running water and dry thoroughly. Remove the stalks from the sorrel, wash and drain. Chop the ham finely.
2. Heat the oil and fry the chopped onions and ham gently for 5 minutes.
3. Set the oven to 190°C (375°F; gas mark 5). Pour the contents of the frying pan into an ovenproof dish, add salt and pepper, cover with one-third of the sorrel, lay the shad on top and season; add the rest of the sorrel and sprinkle with brandy. Cover the dish with buttered paper or foil and bake for 1½ hours.
4. Serve immediately.

Sorrel and brandy are both noted for dissolving the numerous bones of the shad.

Anchois en Tourte
Anchovies Tourtière

Serves 4. Preparation: 20 min Cooking: 30 min

- ○ **1kg (2¼ lb) fresh anchovies**
- ○ **150g (5 oz) breadcrumbs**
- ○ **80g (3 oz) grated Parmesan**
- ○ **2 eggs**
- ○ **30ml (2 tbls) parsley, coarsely chopped**
- ○ **5ml (1 tsp) basil, coarsely chopped**
- ○ **5ml (1 tsp) powdered oregano**
- ○ **60ml (4 tbls) oil**
- ○ **salt and pepper**

1. Cut the heads off the anchovies, clean and wash under cold running water and dry on kitchen paper.
2. Mix the breadcrumbs, grated cheese and herbs in a bowl. Beat the eggs in another bowl with a tablespoon of oil, salt and pepper.
3. Set the oven to 220°C (425°F; gas mark 7). Grease an ovenproof dish and place in it a layer of anchovies, each curled in a circle, with the tail tucked inside. Sprinkle with oil, cover with half of the breadcrumb mixture and season. Proceed with the second layer, using the remaining anchovies, sprinkle with oil and add the rest of the mixture, salt and pepper. Pour over the beaten eggs and bake for 30 minutes.
4. Serve hot.

Instead of Parmesan, this delicious Italian speciality may be prepared with grated Pecorino or goat's milk cheese from the Pyrenees.

A good fish is above all a fresh fish, whether it is the humble whiting, sardine or mackerel, or the noble and expensive turbot, sea-perch or salmon. Never buy a fish whose freshness is in doubt; no subtle dressing or delicate sauce will ever disguise its lack of freshness.

Those lucky enough to buy fish straight from the fishing boats will recognise a fresh fish and its signs: bright eyes, red gills, body rigid and arched; the colours are bright and the scales shining; the flesh is firm and springy and does not give under pressure of a finger; the smell is that of the sea and not of ammonia.

The shad has very delicate flesh in spite of its numerous bones, but deteriorates rapidly. It inhabits the estuaries of large rivers in France and can weigh several pounds.

Anchois Gratinés aux Pommes de Terre

Gratin of Anchovies with Potatoes

Serves 4. Preparation: 30 min
Cooking: 50 min
★★

○ **1kg (2¼ lb) anchovies**
○ **4 large potatoes**
○ **4 ripe tomatoes**
○ **60ml (4 tbls) olive oil**
○ **45ml (3 tbls) parsley, coarsely chopped**
○ **45ml (3 tbls) breadcrumbs**
○ **2 cloves garlic**
○ **salt and pepper**

1. Cut the heads off the anchovies, clean and wash under cold running water and dry on kitchen paper. Divide the fish into fillets, removing the backbone. Peel, wash and cut the potatoes into thin slices.
2. Grease an ovenproof dish, and place in it a layer of anchovies, then one of potatoes; add salt and pepper and sprinkle with oil. Continue adding alternate layers of fish and potatoes, finishing with a layer of fillets.
3. Scald the tomatoes in boiling water for 10 seconds, then refresh in cold water and drain. Skin them, cut in half and remove the seeds. Chop the tomatoes roughly and place on top of the fillets.
4. Set the oven to 220°C (425°F; gas mark 7). Peel the garlic and chop it finely. Add to the tomatoes together with the parsley and the remaining oil, sprinkling the top with breadcrumbs. Bake for 50 minutes.

This dish can also be served cold with a slightly bitter salad, such as endive or dandelion.

Anchois Gratinés aux Aromates

Gratin of Anchovies with Herbs

Serves 4. Preparation: 25 min
Cooking: 25 min
★★

○ **1kg (2¼ lb) anchovies**
○ **4 shallots, finely chopped**
○ **3 cloves garlic**
○ **6 anchovy fillets, canned in oil**
○ **15ml (1 tbls) basil, coarsely chopped**
○ **30ml (2 tbls) parsley, finely chopped**
○ **2.5ml (½ tsp) powdered oregano**
○ **45ml (3 tbls) breadcrumbs**
○ **60g (2 oz) butter**
○ **100ml (3 fl oz) oil**

1. Cut the heads off the anchovies. Clean and wash them under cold running water and dry on kitchen paper. Mash the canned anchovy fillets with a fork.
2. Heat the oil in a saucepan. Add 30g (1 oz) of the butter and then the garlic, shallots, mashed anchovy fillets, parsley and basil. Cook gently for 3 minutes, without letting the mixture brown.
3. Butter an ovenproof dish. Place on it a layer of anchovies and cover with a tablespoon of the mixture. Season with very little salt but plenty of pepper and sprinkle with oregano. Continue with alternate layers, finishing with a layer of anchovies on top.
4. Set the oven to 230°C (450°F; gas mark 8). Melt the remaining butter and pour it over the anchovies. Sprinkle with breadcrumbs and bake for 20 minutes. Serve hot.

Anchois à la Mignonette

Anchovies with Capers and Olives

Serves 4. Preparation: 30 min Cooking: 20 min
★★

○ **1kg (2¼ lb) anchovies**
○ **200ml (7 fl oz) dry white wine**
○ **30ml (2 tbls) capers**
○ **12 black olives, stoned**
○ **45ml (3 tbls) olive oil**
○ **15ml (1 tbls) pepper**
○ **salt**

1. Cut the heads off the anchovies. Clean and wash them under cold running water and dry on kitchen paper. Split the fish open without separating the two fillets and remove the backbone.
2. Finely chop the capers and olives and salt them lightly. Stuff the anchovies with this mixture and reshape them.
3. Set the oven at 230°C (450°F; gas mark 8). Oil an ovenproof dish and place the anchovies on it in a single layer. Add salt, then sprinkle with the pepper, white wine and the remaining oil. Bake for 20 minutes. Serve hot or cold.

Matelote d'Anguilles
Eels in Red Wine

Serves 6. Preparation: 20 min Cooking: 50 min

★★

- ○ **1.6kg (3½ lb) medium-sized eels**
- ○ **24 small peeled onions**
- ○ **24 button mushrooms**
- ○ **1 bottle red wine**
- ○ **2 cloves garlic**
- ○ **1 sprig thyme**
- ○ **1 small bay leaf**
- ○ **½ oz (1 tbls) flour**
- ○ **80g (3 oz) butter**
- ○ **2.5ml (½ tsp) sugar**
- ○ **salt and pepper**

1. Clean and skin the eels, wash and cut into 5cm (2 inch) lengths. Melt half the butter in a saucepan and gently sauté the onions for about 10 minutes, then lift from the pan with a slotted spoon and reserve.
2. Stir in the flour with a wooden spoon, and add the wine, stirring continuously, then add the cloves of garlic, unpeeled and crushed in the palm of the hand, together with the sugar, salt, pepper, thyme, bay leaf and onions. Allow to simmer for 15 minutes.
3. Meanwhile, remove the mushroom stalks, wash and dry the mushrooms and place in the saucepan.
4. When the wine sauce has cooked for 15 minutes, add the eels and simmer for 20 minutes. Because their flesh is firm and oily eels can be plunged into a boiling sauce and then allowed to cook gently.
5. When the eels are cooked, lift out the pieces with a slotted spoon and place on a serving dish. Keep warm. Reduce the sauce for 5 minutes over a high heat; then remove the thyme, bay leaf and garlic. Turn off the heat and add the remaining butter, allowing it to melt slowly in the sauce by gently moving the saucepan. Pour the sauce over the eels and serve immediately.

You can serve this with croûtons fried in butter. This dish cooked in wine is sometimes called 'meurette'. If you add 150g (5 oz) of lean bacon cut into thin strips and fried with the onions it will become a 'pochouse', to which you can add 2 tablespoons of cream at the last minute.

Carp, pike, tench or bream can be prepared in the same way, separately or together.

Anguilles au Four
Baked Eels

Serves 4. Preparation: 10 min Cooking: 30 min

★

- ○ **1kg (2¼ lb) medium-sized eels**
- ○ **100g (4 oz) butter**
- ○ **100ml (½ cup) oil**
- ○ **3 cloves garlic, peeled**
- ○ **30ml (2 tbls) water**
- ○ **60ml (4 tbls) flour**
- ○ **60ml (4 tbls) coarse salt**
- ○ **salt and pepper**

1. Sprinkle the flour on a plate. Skin the eels, cut off the heads, clean and wash. Cut into 5cm (2 inch) lengths, roll in the flour, shake to remove excess and put aside on a plate.
2. Heat the oil in a frying pan and sauté the pieces of eel for 5 minutes until golden brown, turning continuously; drain well.
3. Set the oven to 220°C (425°F; gas mark 7). Melt the butter in a frying pan and fry the cloves of garlic gently, without browning. Place the pieces of eel in an ovenproof dish and spoon over the butter, garlic and water. Season with salt and pepper. Bake for 20 minutes, and serve immediately.

Eel is appreciated for its rich, firm flesh which can be cooked in many different ways: fried, grilled, boiled (au bleu), with spinach (au vert), in red wine, in pâté or even pickled. Smoked eel is delicious, cut into elegant fillets and served on canapés with a slice of lemon.

Anguilles au Vert à la Flamande
Eels with Spinach

Serves 4. Preparation: 25 min
Cooking: 15 min
★★

○ 1kg (2¼ lb) medium-sized eels
○ 3 shallots
○ 100g (4 oz) sorrel
○ 100g (4 oz) spinach
○ 10 sprigs parsley
○ 6 sprigs chives
○ 3 sprigs chervil
○ 2 leaves sage
○ 1 sprig tarragon
○ 1 sprig thyme
○ 2 mint leaves
○ 1 bay leaf
○ 100ml (½ cup) beer or white wine
○ 100g (4 oz) cream
○ 2 egg yolks
○ 40g (1¾ oz) butter
○ salt and pepper

1. Skin the eels, clean, wash and cut into 4cm (1½ inch) lengths. Dry the pieces on kitchen paper.
2. Remove the stalks from the various herbs. Wash the sorrel and spinach and shred finely. Wash the parsley, chervil, tarragon, sage, mint and chives and chop finely. Peel the shallots and chop finely.
3. Melt the butter in a frying pan, add the pieces of eel and shallots and sauté gently for 5 minutes, until golden brown. Remove the pan from the heat and pour away the butter; return to the heat and add the beer, bay leaf and thyme. Cover the pan and allow to cook slowly for 5 minutes.
4. Remove the bay leaf and thyme and add the remaining herbs. Season with salt and pepper. Cover the pan and simmer for a further 5 minutes. Meanwhile, beat together the cream and egg yolks with a fork in a bowl. Set aside.
5. When the eels are cooked, remove from the heat and quickly add the cream sauce, carefully turning the pieces of eel with a spatula to ensure they are evenly coated. Place eels and sauce in a serving dish and serve at once.

Serve this dish with lemon quarters. You can if you prefer omit the cream and eggs; it will be lighter but just as delicious. You can add other herbs besides the ones mentioned, such as watercress or white nettle – 100g (4 oz) of watercress and 50g (2 oz) of nettle.

Anguille en Cocotte
Eel Casserole

Serves 4. Preparation: 10 min Cooking: 30 min
★★

○ 1 large eel, weighing approximately 1kg (2¼ lb)
○ 100g (4 oz) cream
○ 250ml (9 fl oz) dry white wine
○ 100ml (3½ fl oz) brandy
○ 30g (1¼ oz) butter
○ 30ml (2 tbls) oil
○ 3 anchovy fillets
○ 15ml (1 tbls) parsley
○ 2 sprigs rosemary
○ 1 sprig thyme
○ 1 basil leaf
○ salt and pepper

1. Skin the eel and cut off the head. Clean, wash and dry on kitchen paper. Cut into 5cm (2 inch) lengths.
2. Mash the anchovy fillets with a fork and tie the herbs together.
3. Heat the oil in a casserole, add the butter and anchovies. When the anchovies are softened, add the eel and sauté until golden brown, then add the bouquet garni. Season with salt and pepper. Sprinkle with brandy and set alight. Pour on the white wine, cover the pan and allow to simmer on a low heat for 15 minutes, checking occasionally.
4. After 15 minutes remove the bouquet garni and stir in the cream. Cook for 5 minutes over a high heat until the cream has reduced by a third, then turn off the heat.
5. Arrange the pieces of eel on a serving dish, pour over the sauce and serve at once.

Ideally, eel is best cooked and eaten immediately after being killed and skinned. If the fishmonger kills it for you, do not skin it until just before cooking.

Anguille à la Tomate

Serves 4. Preparation: 15 min Cooking: 40 min

Eel with Tomatoes

★★

○ **1 large eel, weighing approximately 1kg (2¼ lb)**
○ **500g (1 lb 2 oz) tomatoes**
○ **100ml (3½ fl oz) dry white wine**
○ **6 sprigs parsley**
○ **4 sage leaves**
○ **2 sticks celery**
○ **1 bay leaf**
○ **1 clove garlic, peeled**
○ **1 small onion, finely chopped**
○ **50g (2 oz) butter**
○ **45ml (3 tbls) oil**
○ **45ml (3 tbls) flour**
○ **salt and pepper**
○ **nutmeg**

1. Sprinkle the flour on a plate. Skin the eel and cut off its head. Clean and wash it under cold running water and dry on kitchen paper. Cut into 7cm (3 inch) lengths and roll the pieces in flour; shake gently to remove excess flour and place on a separate plate.
2. Scald the tomatoes in boiling water for 10 seconds, then drain and refresh in cold water. Peel and cut in two horizontally. Press to remove the seeds and chop roughly.
3. Heat the oil in a flameproof casserole, add the butter and sauté the onion gently on a low heat, then add the tomatoes and white wine. Season with salt, pepper and nutmeg, cover the pan and allow to simmer on low heat for 15 minutes.
4. Meanwhile, finely chop the celery, bay leaf, sage, parsley and garlic and add to the casserole together with the eel. Stir well, then cover and cook gently on a low heat for 20 minutes, checking occasionally.
5. When the eel is cooked, arrange it on a serving dish, cover with the sauce and serve at once.

This dish can be served with garlic bread.

Anguilles Marinées Grillées

Serves 4. Preparation: 15 min Marinade: 12 hr
Cooking: 10 min

Marinated and Grilled Eels

★★

○ **1kg (2¼ lb) small eels, each one weighing about 6 oz (150g)**
○ **60ml (4 tbls) coarse salt**

For the marinade:
○ **4 sage leaves**
○ **2 basil leaves**
○ **2 small onions**
○ **2 cloves garlic**
○ **1 sprig thyme**
○ **1 sprig rosemary**
○ **1 bay leaf**
○ **120ml (4 fl oz) oil**
○ **salt and pepper**

1. The day before: if the eels are rather small, rub them with coarse salt to remove silt, otherwise skin them, cut off the heads, wash under cold running water and dry on kitchen paper. Cut into 5cm (2 inch) pieces.
2. Prepare the marinade: put the pieces of eel in a deep dish; peel and finely chop the garlic and onion; crumble the thyme, rosemary and bay leaf; chop the basil and sage, and add to the eels. Season well and sprinkle with oil. Mix well, cover and leave to marinate for 12 hours, preferably in the fridge.
3. The next day: light the grill; drain the eels, arrange the pieces on the grill pan and grill for approximately 10 minutes, turning the pieces frequently. The eels are ready when both sides are well browned. Serve hot.

Grilled eel is served with lemon quarters or a spicy sauce.

To skin an eel, make a cut around the head and loosen the skin. Then with a quick movement pull off the skin towards the tail, holding the head, wrapped in a cloth, in your other hand. Separate into fillets or cut into pieces and clean with a knife. Before cooking, it is relatively easy to remove the bones from the back and front fins. Elvers, also called piballes *or* civelles, *are delicious fried or served in an omelette.*

Bar au Vin Blanc

Serves 4. Preparation: 10 min Cooking: 40 min

Bass in White Wine

★★

○ **1.2kg (2½ lb) bass**
○ **250ml (9 fl oz) dry white wine**
○ **100g (4 oz) butter**
○ **1 sprig thyme**
○ **1 bay leaf**
○ **30ml (2 tbls) parsley**
○ **1 small onion**
○ **2 cloves**
○ **salt and pepper**
○ **nutmeg**

1. Scale, clean and rinse the fish under cold running water. Butter an ovenproof dish.
2. Set oven to 200°C (400°F; gas mark 6). Peel and slice the onion in thin rounds and lay in the dish, covering the base. Lay the fish on top, pour in the wine and add the thyme, bay leaf, parsley and cloves. Season with salt, pepper and nutmeg. Cover with foil or buttered paper and bake for 30 minutes.
3. When the fish is cooked, lift it out and place on a serving dish. Strain the cooking liquid into a saucepan and place over a high heat. Reduce to approximately 45ml (3 tbls), then lower the heat and whisk in the remaining butter, cut into small knobs, until the sauce is smooth. Pour the sauce over the fish and serve immediately.

Serve with boiled potatoes, leeks julienne or fresh spinach.

Barbue à la Rhubarbe

Serves 4. Preparation and cooking: 1 hr

Brill with Rhubarb

★★

○ **1.5kg (3¼ lb) brill**
○ **1 onion**
○ **2 shallots**
○ **1 carrot**
○ **30ml (2 tbls) parsley**
○ **250ml (9 fl oz) white wine**
○ **6 rhubarb sticks**
○ **200g (7 oz) cream**
○ **20g (1 oz) butter**
○ **salt and pepper**

1. Fillet the fish and skin it. Put aside the head and bones to make stock.
2. Prepare the stock: wash the head and bones of the brill and put in a pan with white wine and a pint of water; add the peeled onion and carrot cut into slices, together with the parsley. Season slightly with salt; bring to the boil and simmer for 20 minutes on low heat.
3. Meanwhile, peel and cut the rhubarb into 3cm (1 inch) pieces. Blanch in boiling water for 10 minutes, then drain and pass through the fine mesh of a vegetable mill. Put aside.
4. When the stock is ready, strain and put aside. Set the oven to 200°C (400°F; gas mark 6). Peel and finely chop the shallot. Butter an ovenproof dish large enough to contain the brill fillets without overlapping, sprinkle with shallots and lay the fillets on top. Pour over the stock, cover with foil and bake for 15 minutes.
5. When cooked, turn off the oven. Lift out the fillets and arrange them on a serving dish, cover with the rhubarb purée and place the dish in the oven with the door ajar.
6. Set the cooking dish over a high heat and reduce the sauce to 250ml (½ pint) of liquid. Add the cream and reduce further for 1 minute. Season to taste with salt and pepper and strain to remove the shallots. Spoon the sauce over the fish and serve immediately.

The tart, fragrant rhubarb adds delicacy to this dish, and today is used more often than sorrel. This recipe is also suitable for turbot, dab and bass.

Bar au Gingembre

Bass in Ginger

Serves 4. Preparation and cooking: 50 min

★★★

○ **1.2kg (2 lb) bass**
○ **1 lemon**

For the marinade:
○ **15ml (1 tbls) soya sauce**
○ **15ml (1 tbls) flour**
○ **15ml (1 tbls) sweet white wine**
○ **2.5ml (½ tsp) powdered ginger**
○ **salt and pepper**

For the sauce:
○ **90ml (6 tbls) oil**
○ **30ml (2 tbls) sweet white wine**
○ **5ml (1 tsp) sugar**
○ **2 leeks (white part only)**
○ **100ml (3½ fl oz) hot water**
○ **1 chicken stock cube**
○ **1 root of ginger 3-4cm**
  (1-1½ inch)
○ **salt**

1. Scale the fish, clean, rinse under cold running water and dry. Place in a dish, season with salt and sprinkle with lemon juice; leave for 10 minutes, turning once.
2. Prepare the marinade: whisk the soya sauce and white wine together with the ginger and flour. Season with salt and pepper. Make small cuts along the back of the fish and pour the marinade over it. Leave to marinade for approximately 15 minutes, turning several times.
3. Prepare the sauce: dissolve the stock cube in hot water, add the white wine and sugar; season and put aside.
4. Grate the ginger; wash and cut the leeks into thin slices. Heat the oil in a frying pan and sauté the leeks and ginger gently for 10 minutes, then lift out, reserving the oil to cook the fish.
5. Drain the fish and fry gently over low heat for 3 minutes on each side. Pour the sauce over it and add the ginger and leeks. Cover and allow to simmer for 15 minutes, turning the fish once. Arrange the bass on a serving dish with the ginger and leek sauce and serve immediately.

Thin slices of chinese mushrooms, or button mushrooms can be added to the leeks.

Barbue à la Tomate et à la Crème

Brill with Tomato and Cream

Serves 4. Preparation and cooking: 45 min

★★

○ **4 brill fillets, weighing 200g**
  (7 oz) each
○ **100g (4 oz) cream**
○ **500g (1 lb 2 oz) tomatoes**
○ **2 large onions, finely chopped**
○ **100ml (3½ fl oz) sweet white**
  wine
○ **45ml (3 tbls) flour**
○ **30ml (2 tbls) parsley, coarsely**
  chopped
○ **40g (1¾ oz) butter**
○ **1 lemon**
○ **oil for frying**
○ **salt and pepper**

1. Rinse the fillets under running water, dry and lay in a dish; sprinkle with lemon juice and leave to marinate for 30 minutes.
2. Meanwhile, scald the tomatoes in boiling water for 10 seconds then drain, refresh in cold water and peel. Cut into halves, remove the seeds and crush to a pulp.
3. Melt the butter in a saucepan, sauté the onions until golden then add the tomatoes. Season with salt and pepper. Allow to cook gently for 15 minutes.
4. Lift out the fillets and roll them in flour. Heat the oil in a frying pan and sauté the fillets for 3 minutes on each side. Remove them, drain and put aside.
5. Add the wine and cream to the tomato sauce, mixing well. Allow to cook for 3 more minutes, then add the fillets to the sauce to simmer for 2 minutes. Arrange the fish on a serving dish, pour the sauce over, sprinkle with parsley and serve at once.

This fish is called by several different names in France: loup *in the Mediterranean,* louvine *or* loubine *on the Basque coast,* drenek *in Britanny. However, it is all the same fish, with delicate, succulent flesh which can be prepared in many ways. It is best grilled with its scales still on – no cleaning or washing – and served with melted butter or a sprinkling of olive oil. Cooked like that, its taste has no equal: protected by the scales, the flesh is cooked without being dried out and the only aroma it gives off is that of the sea . . .*

Baudroie à la Sétoise

Serves 4. Preparation and cooking: 40 min

Angler with Vegetables

★ ★

○ **4 slices of angler or lotte, approximately 250g (9 oz) each**
○ **10 celery leaves**
○ **2 leeks (white part only)**
○ **the green part of 2 beets**
○ **1 carrot**
○ **45ml (3 tbls) olive oil**
○ **salt and pepper**

For the aioli:
○ **1 clove garlic**
○ **1 egg yolk**
○ **2.5ml (½ tsp) mustard**
○ **150ml (6 fl oz) olive oil**
○ **salt**

1. Rinse the fish under cold water and dry on kitchen paper.
2. Wash and peel the carrots, leeks, beet and celery and chop finely.
3. Heat the oil in a saucepan and sauté the vegetables gently for 5 minutes without letting them brown. Season with salt and pepper. Add the slices of fish, cover and simmer over low heat for 20 minutes, turning them once.
4. Meanwhile, prepare the aioli: peel and crush the garlic in a mortar and add the mustard and egg yolk, mixing well. Beat the oil in gradually, little by little, and season with a little salt.
5. When the fish is cooked, remove 45ml (3 tbls) of the cooking juices – this fish gives out a lot of liquid – and stir it into the mortar. Arrange the fish and its cooking juices on a serving dish and spoon the sauce over it. Serve immediately.

Serve with small boiled potatoes and croûtons fried in oil or butter. If you can get the liver of the fish, add it to the saucepan for the last 10 minutes of cooking time. When the fish is cooked, lift out the liver, mash it with a fork and mix with the aioli.

Baudroie au Lait et à la Crème

Serves 4. Preparation and cooking: 30 min approximately

Angler with Milk and Cream

★

○ **4 slices of angler or lotte, approximately 250g (9 oz) each**
○ **250ml (9 fl oz) milk**
○ **125g (4 oz) cream**
○ **1 bay leaf**
○ **45ml (3 tbls) parsley**
○ **5ml (1 tsp) thyme**
○ **1 clove**
○ **1 onion, finely chopped**
○ **50g (2 oz) butter**
○ **20g (¾ oz) flour**
○ **salt and pepper**
○ **nutmeg**

1. Wash the slices of angler under cold running water and dry on kitchen paper.
2. Pour the milk into a saucepan and add the bay leaf, parsley, thyme, onion and clove. Bring to the boil and simmer for 2 minutes. Remove from the heat and strain the milk through a sieve.
3. Melt the butter in another saucepan and stir in the flour with a wooden spoon. Pour in the flavoured milk and cream. Season with salt, pepper and nutmeg. Bring to the boil then add the slices of fish. Cover and simmer gently for 20 minutes over low heat. Arrange the fish on a serving dish and serve at once.

This dish can be served with thin slices of lemon and fresh spinach sautéed in butter.

Brill, which is often mistaken for turbot, is less delicate and not so highly prized, but nevertheless it is succulent, and can be prepared in the same way. It differs from turbot in that its shape is more oval and elongated; the skin is smooth. It can reach up to 80cm (3 ft) in length!

The angler can also be called diable de mer *(sea devil),* grenouille pêcheuse *(fishing frog),* crapaud de mer *(sea toad),* maranche *etc. It is almost always sold headless, and sometimes skinned, under the name of angler tail. It can be as long as 2m (6 ft) and with its round head, enormous for the size of its body, it resembles a huge toad, with numerous pointed teeth. Its flesh is boneless, white and succulent and tastes rather like lobster, but it reduces considerably when cooked. Allow 250 to 400g (9 to 14 oz) per person. The tail when it is whole looks like a leg of lamb, hence its other name: 'gigot de mer'.*

Baudroie Gratinée à la Crème
Angler Gratin with Cream

Serves 4.
Preparation and cooking: 45 min approximately
★

○ **8 slices of angler**
○ **50g (2 oz) butter**
○ **3 onions**
○ **1 clove garlic**
○ **2 eggs**
○ **200ml (7 fl oz) milk**
○ **100ml (4 fl oz) cream**
○ **salt and pepper**
○ **nutmeg**

1. Rinse the fish under cold running water and dry on kitchen paper. Peel the garlic and onion and chop finely.
2. Melt the butter in a frying pan, sauté the fish for 1 minute on each side, then place in an ovenproof dish large enough to contain the fish without overlapping. Season with salt and pepper; add the nutmeg and cover with the chopped garlic and onion.
3. Set the oven to 190°C (375°F; gas mark 5). Beat the eggs in a bowl and stir in the cream and milk. Pour the mixture over the fish and bake for 30 minutes. Serve at once in the same dish.

Serve with small grilled tomatoes or green beans in butter.

Gigot de Lotte à l'Ail Rose
Tail of Angler with Pink Garlic

Serves 4.
Preparation: 15 min Cooking: 25 min
★

○ **1 tail of angler, weighing approximately 1.2kg (2½ lb)**
○ **1 head of pink garlic**
○ **2.5ml (½ tsp) thyme**
○ **1 bay leaf**
○ **2.5ml (½ tsp) fennel seeds**
○ **100ml (3½ fl oz) oil**
○ **1 lemon**
○ **salt and pepper**

1. Set the oven to 220°C (425°F; gas mark 7). Skin the fish, wash and dry it, and tie it up as for a leg of lamb.
2. Peel two cloves of garlic and chop in thin slices. Insert into the flesh of the fish, as for a leg of lamb.
3. Heat the oil in a flameproof dish, sauté the fish gently for 5 minutes, letting it colour evenly on all sides, then remove from the heat.
4. Squeeze the lemon juice onto the fish, dust with thyme and fennel, and season with salt and pepper. Place the rest of the cloves of garlic around the fish, add the bay leaf and bake for 20 minutes. Baste frequently.
5. Once cooked, arrange the fish on a serving dish, remove the string, place the roasted garlic around the fish for everyone to help themselves, pour on the cooking liquid and serve immediately.

A suggested way of serving *gigot de lotte* is with fresh spinach, grilled tomatoes, *lace* potatoes, or braised fennel. Pink garlic comes from Provence and has the most delicate and perfumed of flavours, it is also much more easily digested. Try preparing this dish with fresh garlic, you will be pleasantly surprised at its fine flavour.

Always make sure that you buy angler fish with its skin intact – its delicate soft flesh is damaged by contact with ice, destroying its fine taste and consistency which is similar to that of lobster. It is better to skin the fish yourself or to ask the fishmonger to do it for you.

There is another type of angler, a freshwater fish whose latin name lota lota *is easy to remember, and which inhabits still waters in Central Europe and Eastern France. Its tender, oily, succulent flesh and white liver are highly praised. Like the sea fish it must be skinned before being prepared, whether baked in the oven, cooked in red wine, with cream or simply fried.*

With fish sold headless like the angler or the roussette, *it is easy to check freshness: the flesh should be pale pink and pearly, never blotched red or yellow.*

Brochet à la Crème et aux Noix

Pike with Cream and Walnuts

Serves 4. Preparation: 10 min
Cooking: 15 min
★

○ **4 fillets of pike, approximately 200g (7 oz) each**
○ **80g (3 oz) butter**
○ **100ml (3½ fl oz) white vermouth (Noilly, for example)**
○ **24 green walnuts**
○ **200g (7 oz) cream**
○ **salt and pepper**

1. Roughly chop the walnuts. Rinse the fillets under running cold water and dry them on kitchen paper.
2. Melt the butter in a frying pan and sauté the fillets for 1 minute on each side over a very low heat to prevent the butter burning. Season with salt and pepper and sprinkle with the vermouth. When the liquid has reduced, add the chopped walnuts and cream and cook very slowly over low heat for 10 minutes.
3. Arrange the fillets on a serving dish, pour over the walnut and cream sauce and serve at once.

Sauté de Brochet aux Champignons

Sauté of Pike with Mushrooms

Serves 4. Preparation: 15 min
Cooking: 15 min
★★

○ **1 pike, weighing approximately 1.2kg (2½ lb)**
○ **250g (9 oz) button mushrooms**
○ **100ml (3½ fl oz) brandy**
○ **2 egg yolks**
○ **30g (1 oz) butter**
○ **45ml (3 tbls) cream**
○ **15ml (1 tbls) flour**
○ **15ml (1 tbls) herbs, coarsely chopped**
○ **1 lemon**
○ **salt and pepper**
○ **nutmeg**

1. Clean and scale the pike and cut off the head. Cut into slices 4cm (1½ inches) thick. Rinse and dry on kitchen paper. Dust with flour and shake to remove excess. Cut off the mushroom stalks, rinse and chop into thin slices. Place them in a dish and sprinkle with lemon juice.
2. Melt the butter, sauté the slices of fish lightly for no more than 2 minutes, then add the brandy. When the liquid has reduced, add the mushrooms and season with salt, pepper and nutmeg. Cover and allow to simmer for 6 to 8 minutes, turning frequently, until the mushrooms have rendered all their liquid.
3. Meanwhile, beat the yolks and cream together with a fork.
4. When the fish and mushrooms are cooked, stir in the egg and cream mixture and cook for 2 to 3 minutes. The moment it begins to bubble, take it off the heat at once.
5. Arrange the fish with its sauce on a serving dish, sprinkle with herbs and serve immediately.

The flesh of the barbel is white and succulent, but beware of the bones! Barbel can be prepared in many ways, grilled, fried or cooked in wine. Its flesh, like many freshwater fish, is rather insipid, and it must be served with highly seasoned sauces.

The bonito, similar to a small tuna, can be found in almost all the oceans around the world. Its flesh is red, firm and tasty. It can be baked whole in the oven, with herbs and olive oil, or cooked in a court-bouillon (seasoned stock) and served cold in fillets moistened with olive oil and garnished with capers and gherkins. The boniton is smaller and even tastier than the bonito, but can be found only in the Mediterranean.

Bream has the same kind of flesh and number of bones as barbel. It is ideal for soups.

Pike is prepared mostly in dumplings (quenelles) or stuffed, but it is also delicious cooked in wine, au bleu (boiled in stock) or au vert (with spinach). Its white flesh is succulent, but make sure the fish is a young one; old pike are full of bones. The best pike is found in fast-flowing water; prepare it á la Nantaise, in stock with a little vinegar, and accompany it with beurre blanc – melted butter, beaten in reduced vinegar. See recipe for Sandre au Beurre Blanc, pike-perch in melted butter, page 57.

Cabillaud aux Câpres

Serves 4. Preparation: 10 min Cooking: 8 min

Cod with Capers

★

- ○ **4 cod steaks, weighing approximately 200g (7 oz) each**
- ○ **80g (3 oz) capers**
- ○ **50g (2 oz) black olives**
- ○ **250g (9 oz) ripe tomatoes**
- ○ **15ml (1 tbls) basil, coarsely chopped**
- ○ **90ml (6 tbls) olive oil**
- ○ **salt and pepper**

1. Rinse the cod steaks under cold water and dry on kitchen paper. Stone the olives and chop finely.
2. Scald the tomatoes in boiling water for 10 seconds. Drain, refresh in cold water and peel. Cut into halves, remove the seeds and mash roughly with a fork.
3. Set the oven to 220°C (425°F; gas mark 7). Oil an ovenproof dish with 30ml (2 tbls) olive oil, lay the steaks in the dish and dust with basil, then add the olives, capers and tomatoes. Season with salt and pepper. Sprinkle over the rest of the oil and bake for 20 minutes.
4. Serve hot in the cooking dish.

Basil can be replaced by parsley, oregano, savory or rosemary.

Cabillaud aux Légumes Nouveaux

Serves 4. Preparation: 25 min
Cooking: 30 min

Cod with Fresh Vegetables

★

- ○ **2 cod steaks, 400g (14 oz) each**
- ○ **250g (9 oz) fresh peas**
- ○ **250g (9 oz) new carrots**
- ○ **12 small fresh onions (or pickling onions)**
- ○ **300g (11 oz) ripe tomatoes**
- ○ **60ml (4 tbls) oil**
- ○ **salt and pepper**

1. Rinse the steaks and dry on kitchen paper. Season with salt and pepper. Peel, wash and finely chop the onions and carrots and shell the peas.
2. Scald the tomatoes in boiling water for 10 seconds, peel and cut into halves. Remove seeds and crush roughly. Put aside.
3. Oil a deep saucepan with 15ml (1 tbls) oil. Arrange the fish in the pan, covered by a layer of onions, a layer of carrots, a layer of peas and finally a layer of tomatoes. Season and sprinkle over the rest of the oil. Cover tightly and simmer over moderate heat for 30 minutes without lifting the lid.
4. At the end of the cooking time, carefully mix together the vegetables and the fish and cook for a further 5 minutes with the lid off. Serve immediately.

Tuna or hake could be substituted for cod.

Fresh cod is excellent and can be prepared in many ways. Salted, it becomes morue; *salted and dried,* morue sèche.

Cod is appreciated for its famous liver, its roe, which can be salted and smoked, and its tongue. Fishermen are traditionally given the right to remove the cod tongues themselves, which is apparently the best part of the fish. These tongues can be eaten fresh, fried or pickled.

In international gastronomy carp has quite a reputation. Very popular in the Middle Ages it seems to be less so today, although it is a fish of exquisite taste with a delicate roe which can be prepared à la meunière *(fried in butter), baked in the oven with* beurre blanc, *sautéed with red wine and mushrooms, cooked Jewish style (sweet and sour) or stuffed.*

Cabillaud Grillé au Beurre d'Anchois

Grilled Cod with Anchovy Butter

Serves 4. Preparation: 10 min
Cooking: 8 min
★

- ○ **4 cod steaks, 200g (7 oz) each**
- ○ **100g (4 oz) butter**
- ○ **15ml (1 tbls) anchovy paste**
- ○ **15ml (1 tbls) capers**
- ○ **½ lemon**
- ○ **30ml (2 tbls) oil**
- ○ **salt and pepper**

1. Heat the grill. Wash the steaks under cold running water, dry, season with salt and sprinkle with oil. Finely chop the capers.
2. When the grill is hot, cook the fish for 3 to 4 minutes on both sides.
3. Meanwhile, melt the butter in a saucepan and add the anchovy paste, lemon juice and capers. Season with pepper, mix well and take off the heat.
4. Arrange the fish on a serving dish, pour over the sauce and serve at once.

Serve this dish with sautéed courgettes or aubergines.

Carpe à la Juive

Carp Jewish-Style

Serves 4. Preparation: 15 min Cooking: 45 min

- ○ **1 carp, weighing about 1.5kg (3¼ lb)**
- ○ **3 onions**
- ○ **2 shallots**
- ○ **2 cloves garlic**
- ○ **30ml (2 tbls) flour**
- ○ **200ml (7 fl oz) oil**
- ○ **1 litre (35 fl oz) white wine**
- ○ **1 bouquet garni: parsley, bay leaf, thyme**
- ○ **30ml (2 tbls) parsley, coarsely chopped**
- ○ **salt and pepper**

1. Clean and scale the fish and cut into thick slices. Peel the onions and shallots and chop finely. Tie up the bouquet garni and crush the garlic.
2. Heat half the oil in a large saucepan and cook the onions and shallots gently for 10 minutes. Add the fish and fry rapidly for 1 minute on both sides; dust with flour and cook gently for 2 minutes on each side, without browning. Add the garlic, bouquet garni and wine and cover with cold water. Season with salt and pepper. Bring to the boil, cover and allow to simmer for 25 minutes.
3. When cooked, drain the slices and transfer to an oval dish, carefully arranging them so as to reshape the fish.
4. Reduce the sauce to one-third by boiling over a high heat and remove the bouquet garni. Draw aside and stir in the rest of the oil, beating vigorously until the sauce is frothy. Adjust the seasoning if necessary and pour over the carp.
5. Allow to cool: the sauce will turn to a jelly. Sprinkle with chopped parsley before serving.

There are many ways of preparing this dish. Carp Jewish-style with parsley – add a large bunch of parsley while cooking; sweet and sour – add to the sauce 15ml (1 tbls) of sugar, 45ml (3 tbls) of alcohol vinegar, 100g (4 oz) of raisins or sultanas soaked in warm water; or oriental-style – add 60ml (4 tbls) of grated almonds and a pinch of saffron.

Suitable for pike or pike-perch.

Plaice belongs to the turbot and brill family. This succulent white fish is particularly recommended for invalids as it is fat-free and easy to digest. It is an attractive flat fish dotted with orange. Plaice can be prepared like turbot or brill: the smallest fried in butter à la meunière, the biggest poached whole or in fillets.

Dorade en Papillote

Dorado with Shellfish

Serves 4. Preparation: 15 min Cooking: 45 min

★

○ **1 dorado, approximately 1.2kg (2½ lb)**
○ **20 clams**
○ **10 mussels**
○ **10 Dublin Bay prawns (langoustines)**
○ **1 finely chopped onion**
○ **10 sprigs of parsley**
○ **1 lemon**
○ **60ml (4 tbls) oil**
○ **salt and pepper**

1. Clean, scale and rinse the fish under cold running water and dry on kitchen paper. Rinse the prawns and clams and scrub the mussels, then rinse.
2. Set the oven to 220°C (425°F; gas mark 7) and chop the parsley finely.
3. Take a sheet of foil large enough to contain the fish and shellfish. Put on the bottom the onion and parsley, then the dorado, and season with salt and pepper. Arrange the clams, mussels and prawns around the fish and sprinkle with the lemon juice and 45ml (3 tbls) of oil. Close tightly by twisting the edges together.
4. Place the parcel on an oiled baking sheet and bake for 45 minutes. Serve with quarters of lemon.

Dorade à la Tahitienne

Dorado Tahiti-Style

Serves 4. Preparation: 30 min Marinade: 2 hr

★

○ **1 dorado, approximately 1.5kg (3¼ lb)**
○ **6 green lemons**
○ **150ml (¼ pint) coconut milk**
○ **salt and pepper**

To serve:
○ **4 new small onions or a bunch of chives**
○ **1 lettuce**
○ **4 small tomatoes**

1. Ask the fishmonger to cut the fish into fillets. Dry with kitchen paper and check that no bones are left.
2. Cut the fillets in halves lengthwise and then into thin slices. Place in a salad bowl.
3. Squeeze the lemons and sprinkle the fillets with the lemon juice; season with salt and pepper and mix well before placing the bowl in the fridge for at least 2 hours, turning occasionally.
4. 15 minutes before serving, peel the small onions and chop finely with the chives. Remove four large leaves and the heart from the lettuce and shred the rest finely. Rinse the tomatoes, dry and cut in thin slices.
5. When it is time to serve, place the lettuce on a serving dish, the heart in the centre and the large leaves around it. Lift the fish from its marinade and arrange on the bed of lettuce. Pour over the coconut milk.
6. Garnish with the onions and tomatoes and serve at once.

This recipe is suitable for fillets of bass, sole and turbot; add the juice of a garlic clove to the marinade. Non-sweetened coconut milk is easier to find nowadays but if you prefer preparing it yourself proceed as follows: grate the coconut meat, placing it in a mixer with the same weight of water, milk or cream and blend until you have a purée. Push through a fine sieve and keep in the fridge. Otherwise, coconut milk can be replaced by cream.

This dorado Tahiti-style is not raw fish: the salt and lemon juice of the marinade literally cook it.

Dorade au Sel
Dorado with Salt

Serves 4. Preparation: 10 min Cooking: 45 min

★

○ **1 dorado, approximately 1.2kg (2½ lb)**
○ **1.5kg (3 lb) coarse salt**
○ **1 bunch parsley**

For the sauce:
○ **90ml (6 tbls) olive oil**
○ **1 lemon**
○ **1 clove garlic**
○ **45ml (3 tbls) herbs: parsley, chervil, chives, basil, tarragon, coarsely chopped**
○ **salt and pepper**

1. Do not scale the fish, just clean, rinse and dry on kitchen paper. Stuff with parsley to prevent the salt getting inside. Set the oven to 230°C (450°F; gas mark 8).
2. Put half the coarse salt in an ovenproof dish, place the fish on top and cover with the rest of the salt. Bake for 45 minutes.
3. Meanwhile, prepare the sauce: peel and crush the garlic and place the juice in a bowl; add the lemon juice, season with salt and pepper and stir in the oil, mixing vigorously. Add the herbs to the mixture.
4. When the fish is cooked, lift it out of the dish and break open the salt crust that has formed. The skin of the fish will come away with the crust, revealing the dorado perfectly cooked and moist.
5. Separate into fillets and arrange on individual plates. Serve the sauce separately.

It is possible also to bring the whole fish to the table and prepare it in front of your guests. When in season, you can add the pulp of two large tomatoes to the sauce.

This recipe is also suitable for bass and mullet. Fish cooked in this way must be extremely fresh.

Dorade aux Poivrons Rouges
Dorado with Red Peppers

Serves 4. Preparation: 15 min
Cooking: 55 min
★ ★

○ **1 dorado, approximately 1.2kg (2½ lb)**
○ **250g (9 oz) onions, finely chopped**
○ **2 red peppers**
○ **80g (3 oz) butter**
○ **200ml (7 fl oz) dry white wine**
○ **150g (5 oz) cream**
○ **250ml (½ pint) hot water**
○ **1 stock cube**
○ **15ml (1 tbls) tomato purée**
○ **15ml (1 tbls) flour**
○ **5ml (1 tsp) paprika**
○ **salt**

1. Scale and clean the fish. Rinse under cold running water and dry on kitchen paper. Season with salt on both sides and inside.
2. Rinse the peppers, cut lengthwise in four pieces and remove the centre, seeds and white filaments. Cut each quarter into thin slices. Dissolve the stock cube in hot water.
3. Heat the butter in a saucepan and gently sauté the onions and peppers for 5 minutes, then add the stock and paprika. Bring to the boil and simmer for 5 minutes before putting in the dorado. Season with salt, cover and cook gently for 15 minutes. Turn the fish over and leave to cook for a further 15 minutes.
4. When ready, lift out the dorado and keep warm on a serving dish. Dilute the tomato purée with the white wine and pour into the saucepan. Boil rapidly for 5 minutes to reduce the sauce by half.
5. Meanwhile, mix the flour with 15ml (1 tbls) of water and add to the sauce, stirring continuously with a wooden spoon. Allow to cook for 5 minutes and then add the cream. Bring to the boil then remove from the heat. Coat the fish with the sauce and serve at once.

The conger eel is also called the sea eel because of its shape. It can reach up to 1½m (4 ft) in length and weigh up to 6kg (14 lb). Not as refined as the river eel, it is used mainly for soups, bouillabaisses, bourrides *(Provençal cookery) and* matelotes *(cooked in wine).*

Filets de Dorade au Citron Vert

Fillets of Dorado with Lime

Serves 4. Preparation and cooking: 1 hr

★ ★ ★

○ **2 dorados, approximately 600g (1½ lb) each**
○ **15ml (1 tbls) coriander leaves, coarsely chopped**
○ **2 shallots**
○ **60g (2 oz) butter**
○ **1 lime**
○ **juice of one lime**

For the stock:
○ **150ml (5 fl oz) dry white wine**
○ **1 medium-sized onion**
○ **1 carrot**
○ **1 bouquet garni: bay leaf, thyme, celery stick**
○ **salt**
○ **6 peppercorns**

1. Scale and clean the fish and divide into fillets. Keep the heads and bones for stock.
2. Prepare the stock: peel the onion and carrot and slice finely. Tie the bouquet garni and place in a saucepan together with the heads and bones, the carrot, onion, pepper and wine. Cover with ½ litre (1 pint) of cold water and bring to the boil. Season with salt, cover and simmer for 20 minutes.
3. Meanwhile, peel the shallots and chop finely. Add the coriander and place the mixture in an ovenproof dish. Arrange the fillets on top. Set the oven to 220°C (425°F; gas mark 7).
4. When the stock is ready, strain over the fillets, cover with foil and bake for 15 minutes, basting the fillets occasionally.
5. When the fish is cooked, lift out and arrange on a serving dish; keep warm. Place the cooking dish on a high heat and boil down the cooking liquid to 200ml (7 fl oz) approximately. Remove from heat and add the lime juice and then the butter, cut into small knobs, beating until the sauce is smooth. Pour the sauce over the fillets, garnish with slices of lime and serve immediately.

If you cannot find fresh coriander, replace with parsley or tarragon.

Dorade aux Fines Herbes

Dorado with Herbs

Serves 4. Preparation: 10 min Cooking: 30 min

★

○ **1 dorado, 1.2kg (2½ lb)**
○ **1 sprig thyme**
○ **2 sprigs fennel**
○ **15ml (1 tbls) parsley, coarsely chopped**
○ **1 bay leaf**
○ **3 onions (pickling onions)**
○ **200ml (7 fl oz) dry white wine**
○ **45ml (3 tbls) oil**
○ **salt and pepper**

1. Scale, clean and rinse the fish under cold running water and dry on kitchen paper.
2. Set the oven to 220°C (425°F; gas mark 7). Chop the fennel and onions finely, and oil an ovenproof dish with 15ml (1 tbls) oil. Season the inside of the fish with salt and pepper and insert the bay leaf and thyme. Lay the fish in the oven dish and add a little salt, surround with the chopped onions, sprinkle with oil and bake for 10 minutes.
3. After 10 minutes pour the wine over and cook for another 15 minutes. Sprinkle with parsley and fennel, cook for 5 minutes and serve immediately.

The dorado is one of the best sea fish but much more difficult to find than one thinks, as many dorados sold on the market are not always the real ones!

The true dorado, with its dark blue back and silver sides, has a characteristic yellow spot on each side of its head and a crescent shaped mark on the forehead, between the two eyes – it looks like a crown and a pair of golden glasses. That is the royal dorado, or dorado with golden eyebrows! Its flesh is delicate and succulent, rare and very expensive. To appreciate it fully, prepare it simply: grilled with its scales, like the bass, en papillote (in foil), or baked in salt.

Dorade Gratinée à la Vénitienne

Gratin of Dorado Venetian-Style

Serves 4. Marinade: 30 min
Preparation: 15 min Cooking: 35 min
★★

○ **1 dorado, weighing approximately 1.5kg (3¼ lb)**
○ **1 400g (14 oz) tin peeled tomatoes**
○ **100ml (3½ fl oz) dry white wine**
○ **150g (5 oz) black olives**
○ **6 anchovy fillets in oil**
○ **25g (1 oz) capers in vinegar**
○ **10 sprigs parsley**
○ **5ml (1 tsp) oregano**
○ **1 clove garlic**
○ **juice of 1 lemon**
○ **90ml (6 tbls) oil**
○ **salt and pepper**

1. Scale and clean the fish. Rinse under cold running water and dry on kitchen paper. Season with salt inside and on both sides. Place in a dish, sprinkle with lemon juice and marinate for 30 minutes, turning once.
2. Meanwhile, peel the garlic and stone the olives; finely chop the garlic, parsley, capers, anchovies and olives, all of them separately. Cut the tomatoes in halves, reserving the juice, remove the seeds and crush to a pulp with a fork.
3. Heat 45ml (3 tbls) of oil in a saucepan, add the garlic, parsley, anchovies and capers. Gently sauté for approximately 5 minutes, sprinkle with half the white wine, then allow it to evaporate. Add the tomatoes and their juice, cook for 5 minutes over a high heat and add the olives. Season with salt and pepper and remove from the heat.
4. Set the oven to 220°C (425°F; gas mark 7). Oil a baking dish with 30ml (2 tbls) of oil, drain the fish and lay it in. Pour the sauce over with the rest of the wine. Dust with oregano and add the remaining oil. Bake for 20 minutes and serve at once.

Dorade Bercy

Dorado Bercy (baked with herbs)

Serves 4. Preparation: 10 min Cooking: 35 min
★

○ **1 dorado, 1.2kg (2½ lb)**
○ **2 sprigs thyme**
○ **2 bay leaves**
○ **1 sprig fennel**
○ **60g (2 oz) butter**
○ **3 shallots**
○ **100ml (3½ fl oz) oil**
○ **30ml (2 tbls) parsley, coarsely chopped**
○ **200ml (7 fl oz) dry white wine**
○ **salt and pepper**

1. Scale, clean and rinse the fish under cold running water. Dry on kitchen paper. Season with salt and pepper and place the thyme, fennel and bay leaves inside the fish.
2. Set the oven to 220°C (425°F; gas mark 7). Peel and chop the shallots finely.
3. Butter an ovenproof dish with 20g (¾ oz) of the butter and cover the base with the shallots. Place the dorado on top and sprinkle with the wine and oil. Bake for 35 minutes, basting frequently.
4. Meanwhile, mash the remaining butter with the parsley. When the fish is cooked, dot with knobs of butter and serve immediately in the same dish.

This dish can be served with small steamed potatoes, braised fennel or a salad of warm courgettes.

There are other types of dorado, more common and less expensive but still very tasty: the pageot *or pink dorado and the* griset *or sea bream. These fish have the same shape as the real dorado, but the first has a black spot on each side of the gills, a grey back and pink sides, and the second is silvery with golden lines on its sides. The best dorado comes from the Mediterranean and the Gulf of Gascony.*

When you buy a fish, ask the fishmonger to scale, clean and cut it into fillets. If you decide to do it yourself, use a scaling knife, a pair of scissors, and a small knife with a short pointed blade for cutting the fillets.

Dorade aux Fines Herbes (p25) ▶

Ragoût de Dorade aux Aromates
Stewed Dorado with Herbs

Serves 4. Preparation: 20 min
Cooking: 45 min
★★

○ **1 dorado, 1.2kg (2½ lb)**
○ **1 stick of celery**
○ **1 carrot**
○ **1 medium-sized onion**
○ **1 clove garlic**
○ **10 sprigs parsley**
○ **3 sage leaves**
○ **1 bay leaf**
○ **60ml (4 tbls) oil**
○ **2 salted anchovies**
○ **25g (1 oz) pine kernels**
○ **25g (1 oz) capers**
○ **25g (1 oz) dried mushrooms (dried ceps)**
○ **1 small pimento**
○ **100ml (3½ fl oz) dry white wine**
○ **15ml (1 tbls) tomato purée**
○ **salt and pepper**

1. Scale, clean and rinse the fish under cold running water and dry. Cut into four equal slices.
2. Peel the carrot, onion and garlic and chop finely, together with the celery, parsley and sage. Rinse the anchovies, remove the spine and chop finely. Place the dried mushrooms in boiling water for 3 minutes and then drain.
3. Heat the oil in a casserole and gently sauté the celery, carrot, garlic, onion, parsley and sage. Add the anchovies, pine kernels, capers, mushrooms, bay leaf and the small pimento, crushed between your fingers. Simmer for 5 minutes, stirring well with a wooden spoon, then sprinkle with the white wine, bring to the boil and reduce. Add the tomato purée and water and mix well.
4. Arrange the slices of fish in the casserole, season with salt and pepper and cover. Cook gently for 30 minutes, turning the fish several times. When ready, arrange on a serving dish and serve at once.

This dish can be accompanied with small croûtons rubbed with garlic. This recipe is also suitable for cod, conger eel or a mixture of white fish.

Dorade aux Câpres
Dorado with Capers

Serves 4. Preparation and cooking: 1 hr

★★

○ **1 dorado, 1.2kg (2½ lb)**
○ **70g (3 oz) capers**
○ **100g (4 oz) gherkins**
○ **80g (3½ oz) butter**
○ **1 egg yolk**
○ **15ml (1 tbls) flour**
○ **1 lemon**
○ **salt and pepper**

For the stock:
○ **45ml (3 tbls) vinegar**
○ **1 stick celery**
○ **1 carrot**
○ **1 onion**
○ **1 bouquet garni: 6 sprigs parsley, thyme, bay leaf**
○ **3 cloves**
○ **salt and peppercorns**

1. Prepare the stock: chop the celery, scrape and slice the carrots, peel and spike the onion with cloves. Tie the bouquet garni.
2. Place in a fish kettle 1½ litres (3 pints) of water, the vinegar, celery, carrot, onion, bouquet garni and 5 or 6 peppercorns. Bring to the boil, season with salt and leave to cook gently for 30 minutes.
3. Meanwhile, scale, clean and rinse the fish under cold running water and dry on kitchen paper. When the stock is ready, reduce the heat and add the dorado, cover and allow to simmer over low heat for 20 minutes. The water must not boil.
4. Meanwhile, chop the capers and gherkins finely. Melt the butter in a saucepan, stir in the flour gradually, stirring with a wooden spoon, and slowly add 60ml (4 tbls) of stock. Cook for 10 minutes, stirring continuously. Remove from the heat and add the capers, gherkins and egg yolk. Mix vigorously and season with salt and pepper.
5. Drain the fish, skin it, and separate into fillets. Arrange on a serving dish and coat with the sauce. Serve with slices of lemon.

If you do not possess a fish kettle with a grid, wrap the fish in thin linen and tie it at both ends as en papillote *(in foil).*

Haddock au Lait

Serves 4. Preparation: 5 min Cooking: 15 min

Haddock in Milk

★

○ **800g (2 lb) haddock**
○ **1 litre (1¾ pints) milk**

For the sauce:
○ **100g (4 oz) butter**
○ **juice of 1 lemon**
○ **45ml (3 tbls) capers**
○ **salt and pepper**

1. Rinse the haddock and dry on kitchen paper.
2. Place the fish in a saucepan and cover with the milk. Set on medium heat, bring to the boil, and reduce heat at once to simmer for 10 minutes.
3. Meanwhile, prepare the butter with capers: melt the butter, remove from the heat and add the lemon juice, capers, salt and pepper. Keep warm.
4. When the haddock is cooked, lift it out with a fish slice and place in a serving dish. Serve immediately, handing round the sauce separately.

Haddock au Citron

Serves 4. Preparation: 5 min Cooking: 20 min

Haddock with Lemon

★

○ **800g (2 lb) haddock**
○ **125g (4 oz) butter**
○ **juice of 4 lemons**
○ **salt and pepper**

1. Rinse the fish under cold water and dry on kitchen paper.
2. Place the fish in a saucepan, cover with cold water and bring to the boil. The minute it comes to the boil, remove from the heat and lift out the fish.
3. Meanwhile, set the oven at 170°C (325°F; gas mark 3).
4. Place the fish in an ovenproof dish. Cut the butter into large knobs, dot over the fish and squeeze over the lemon juice. Bake for about 10 minutes. The butter and lemon must be hot, but should not be allowed to boil.
5. Serve the fish very hot, in its cooking dish.

Serve with small steamed potatoes or fresh spinach poached for 3 minutes in boiling water.

The haddock, with its grey sides and white front, has a characteristic black spot near the first back fin. It is also called black cod. Fresh, it is prepared like cod; salted and smoked, it becomes the fish beloved of the English.

The true smoked haddock should be pale yellow, the colour that comes naturally from smoking over a wood fire; if it is darker, more orange, it has been smoked artificially. Often, fillets of ling are sold as haddock. Always ask for real haddock.

The smelt, a small silver fish, is never longer than 25cm (10 inches) and can be deep fried, whole if small, or in fillets when larger. It must not be mistaken for the sand eel which is also tasty but more bland. The smelt, when fresh, has a faint aroma of cucumber, or if less fresh, violet. Always choose the smallest. Clean through the gills, dust with flour, tie up in small bunches and deep fry in hot oil (but not smoking); season with salt, pepper and lemon.

The sturgeon, famous mostly for its roe – caviar – has an extremely succulent flesh when smoked, but it is also excellent braised, grilled or fried. It is found in France in the Rhone and Garonne regions.

The féra, which inhabits Lake Geneva and Lake Constance, tastes much like trout and can be prepared in the same way. In Geneva, féras are served deep fried, the bigger ones in fillets.

Harengs au Bacon

Herrings with Bacon

Serves 4. Preparation: 20 min Cooking: 15 min

★★

○ **8 fresh herrings, each about 150g (5 oz)**
○ **16 slices of bacon**
○ **30ml (2 tbls) mustard**
○ **juice of 1 lemon**
○ **100ml (3½ fl oz) oil**
○ **salt**

1. Scale, clean and rinse the fish under cold running water and dry. Remove the heads, separate into fillets and remove the backbone. Place the fillets on a large plate, sprinkle with lemon juice and season with a little salt. Coat each fillet with mustard, reshape the fish and put 2 slices of bacon around each herring, securing with string or cocktail sticks.
2. Heat the oil in a large frying pan and fry the fish for 5 to 7 minutes on each side. When cooked, drain on kitchen paper before arranging on a serving dish. Serve immediately.

Serve with a green or mixed salad: tomato and cucumber, mushroom and fennel, or red and white cabbage. Small mackerel called *lisettes* can be prepared in the same way.

Harengs Salés au Vin Blanc

Salted Herring with White Wine

Serves 4. Preparation: 10 min Marinade: 2 hr
Cooking: 25 min

★★

○ **8 salted herrings**
○ **250ml (9 fl oz)) dry white wine**
○ **250ml (½ pint) milk**
○ **100ml (3½ fl oz) alcohol vinegar**
○ **60g (2 oz) butter**
○ **1 medium-sized onion**
○ **1 clove garlic**
○ **2.5ml (½ tsp) chopped thyme**
○ **2.5ml (½ tsp) rosemary**
○ **3 sage leaves**
○ **1 bay leaf**
○ **1 celery stick**
○ **10 sprigs parsley**

1. The day before: put the fish to soak in milk for 12 hours.
2. The next day: peel the garlic and onion and chop finely together with the bay leaf, sage, parsley and celery. Drain the fish and dry with kitchen paper to remove all the milk from the marinade.
3. Melt the butter in a frying pan, add the herbs, garlic, onion and celery and fry for 5 minutes. Add the wine and vinegar and boil down to a third of the liquid. Reduce the heat, add the fish and allow to simmer for 10 minutes.
4. Serve hot or cold.

*Flounder resembles plaice, except that its yellow spots are not as obvious. It is slightly longer and can live up to 40 years of age. Its flesh is rather oily and is best prepared in fillets and fried in butter (*à la meunière*).*

Halibut is the largest flat fish. It looks like an enormous plaice and can weigh up to 200kg (440 lb). It is found in northern waters and its firm white flesh is greatly valued and very delicate. It can be prepared in escalopes and baked in the oven, fried, poached or cooked au gratin. *In Northern countries it is often salted or smoked and in Great Britain most fish restaurants offer halibut on their menu.*

Gurnet, often called red mullet, is mistakenly sold as the real mullet but it is quite different to look at and to taste. Although its flesh is quite delicate, this fish with its huge head and many bones is best used in bouillabaisses *and fish soup. Beware of these bones, they can be dangerous. You can tell a gurnet is fresh from its bright colours: red back and white front. If it is pink, don't buy it.*

Gudgeon is a small fish which is to be found in all the lakes and rivers of Europe and is best deep fried. It is delicious.

Lieu Noir en Cocotte

Serves 4. Preparation: 20 min Cooking: 35 min

Stewed Saithe

★

- ○ 900g (2 lb) saithe
- ○ 200ml (7 fl oz) dry white wine
- ○ 150g (6 oz) button mushrooms
- ○ 2 ripe romatoes
- ○ 1 clove garlic
- ○ 1 carrot
- ○ 50g (2 oz) butter
- ○ salt and pepper

1. Scald the tomatoes in boiling water for 10 seconds, drain and refresh in cold water. Peel, cut into halves, remove the seeds and crush to a pulp with a fork.
2. Rinse and dry the fish on kitchen paper. Peel and chop the garlic and onion finely. Scrape the carrot and cut into thin rounds. Remove the stalks of the mushrooms, rinse and chop into thin slices.
3. Melt the butter in a saucepan and sauté the garlic, onion and carrot gently together for 3 minutes. Add the mushrooms and tomatoes, mix well, and pour in the white wine. Add the fish and season with salt and pepper. Cover and cook slowly over low heat for 30 minutes, turning the fish after 15 minutes.
4. Arrange the fish on a serving dish, surround with the carrot and mushrooms, pour the sauce over and serve at once.

Serve with small potato cakes or sautéed courgettes or aubergines.

Lieu Noir aux Olives

Serves 4. Preparation: 15 min Cooking: 40 min

Saithe with Olives

★★

- ○ 900g (2 lb) saithe
- ○ 150g (6 oz) green olives
- ○ 500g (1¼ lb) ripe tomatoes
- ○ 15ml (1 tbls) parsley, coarsely chopped
- ○ 15ml (1 tbls) basil, coarsely chopped
- ○ 1 onion
- ○ 1 carrot
- ○ 1 stick celery
- ○ 1 clove garlic
- ○ 1 bay leaf
- ○ 75ml (5 tbls) oil
- ○ salt and pepper

1. Rinse the fish under running water and dry on kitchen paper.
2. Peel the onion, garlic and carrot and chop, together with the celery.
3. Scald the tomatoes in boiling water for 10 seconds, drain and refresh in cold water, peel and remove the seeds. Crush to a pulp with a fork and reserve.
4. Heat the oil in a saucepan and sauté the garlic and vegetables for 5 minutes on a low heat. When it has all taken on a pale yellow colour, add the fish and sauté for 2 minutes on each side. Add the tomatoes and bay leaf and season with salt and pepper. Cover, and simmer on a low heat for 15 minutes, turning the fish once.
5. Meanwhile, stone the olives and when the 15 minutes cooking time has elapsed add them to the fish, together with the parsley and basil, and leave to cook for a further 15 minutes.
6. When ready, arrange the fish on a serving dish, coat with the olive sauce and serve hot.

This dish may be accompanied with small croûtons rubbed with garlic. When basil is out of season, use half a teaspoon of fennel seeds or oregano.

Yellow or black saithe arrives on the market headless and ready to be cut into steaks — it can weigh up to 10kg (22 lb). It is of the cod family, and its white, delicate flesh is boneless and easily digested.

Cod is the best, then yellow saithe and lastly black saithe. It can be poached either in salted water or in stock with a little vinegar, or cooked in steaks, fried in butter.

Lieu Grillé Sauce aux Câpres

Serves 4. Preparation: 5 min Cooking: 5 min

Grilled Saithe with Caper Sauce

★

○ **4 steaks of saithe, 200g (7 oz) each**
○ **80g (3 oz) butter**
○ **15ml (1 tbls) oil**
○ **5ml (1 tsp) vinegar**
○ **15ml (1 tbls) mustard**
○ **50g (2 oz) capers**
○ **salt and pepper**

1. Heat the grill. Rinse the fish, dry on kitchen paper, oil and season with salt. Grill for 2 minutes on each side.
2. Meanwhile, melt the butter in a saucepan, add the mustard and season with salt and pepper. Sprinkle with vinegar, add the capers, and mix well.
3. When the fish is cooked, arrange on a serving dish, pour over the sauce and serve at once.

Serve with boiled potatoes in their jackets and a green salad.

Limande aux Crevettes Grises

Serves 3-4. Preparation and cooking: 35 min

Dab with Prawns

○ **2 dabs, approximately 500g (1¼ lb) each**
○ **250ml (9 fl oz) dry white wine**
○ **1 small chopped onion**
○ **1 clove**
○ **1 bay leaf**
○ **salt**

For the sauce:
○ **150g (6 oz) prawns, shelled**
○ **50g (2 oz) butter**
○ **20g (¾ oz) flour**
○ **1 egg yolk**
○ **100g (4 oz) cream**
○ **½ lemon**
○ **salt and white pepper**
○ **nutmeg**

1. Scale, clean and rinse the fish under running cold water. Remove heads and tails.
2. Place the wine and ½ litre (18 fl oz) of water in a saucepan large enough to contain the fish without overlapping. Add the onion, clove, bay leaf and the fish. Bring to the boil, season with salt and cover. Allow to simmer for 15 minutes.
3. When ready, lift out the dabs and keep warm on a serving dish. Strain the stock and boil down to a third.
4. Melt the butter in a saucepan, stir in the flour and cook very gently, until it is a pale yellow colour. Blend in the stock gradually, mixing continuously with a wooden spoon, and let it cook for 3 minutes. Remove from the heat.
5. Mix the cream and egg yolk together and add to the sauce. Sprinkle with lemon juice and season with salt, pepper and nutmeg. Add the prawns and stir gently. Pour the sauce over the fish and serve immediately.

You can tell if a fish sold in steaks is fresh – the white flesh should stick to the backbone and there should be no red halo around it.

There are several types of dab: the common or pale dab, the sole dab or limandelle *and the false dab. The colouring varies from light brown to grey, pale yellow or spotted brown. The best is undoubtedly the sole dab, which is similar to the sole in appearance and taste. It can be prepared like the sole or plaice and although its taste is not as delicate, you will appreciate it.*

Ling, also called long cod, is a long fish similar to the conger eel and can reach up to 1½ metres (5 ft). It is fished in the North Sea and sold mostly in fillets or salted. Its flesh is similar to that of the cod; it is rather insipid but very easy to digest. In northern countries, it is either smoked, salted or dried.

Limande au Cidre

Dab with Cider

Serves 3. Preparation: 10 min Cooking: 25 min

★★

○ **1 dab, about 800g (2 lb)**
○ **½-1 bottle of cider**
○ **2 shallots, chopped finely**
○ **1 bunch chives**
○ **125g (5 oz) cream**
○ **50g (2 oz) butter**
○ **salt and pepper**

1. Clean the fish through its gills, without cutting it open.
2. Set the oven to 220°C (425°F; gas mark 7). Butter an ovenproof dish, using half the butter, and scatter with the shallots.
3. Rinse and dry the fish, place it in the dish, season with salt and barely cover with the cider. Dot with the remaining butter and bake for 20 minutes, basting occasionally.
4. When cooked, arrange the fish on a serving dish; cover with foil and put back in the oven. Switch the oven off and leave the door ajar.
5. Place the cooking dish over a high heat and reduce the cooking liquid until you have about 150ml (5 fl oz) left, add the cream, boil for 1 minute and remove from the heat.
6. Chop the chives and add to the sauce, season with pepper and pour the sauce over the dab. Serve at once.

You can serve this dish with boiled potatoes or apples fried in butter. Replace the chives with herbs of your choice and add a few drops of lemon. The same cider should be served to drink.

Suitable for plaice, dorado or bass.

Filets de Limande à la Vapeur

Steamed Dab Fillets

Serves 4. Preparation and cooking: 25 min

★★

○ **8 dab fillets**
○ **1 egg**
○ **2 egg yolks**
○ **15ml (1 tbls) capers**
○ **15ml (1 tbls) gherkins**
○ **15ml (1 tbls) mustard**
○ **10 sprigs parsley**
○ **200ml (7 fl oz) oil**
○ **½ lemon**
○ **salt and pepper**

1. Rinse the fillets under cold water and dry. Oil and season with salt and pepper. Wrap each fillet in foil and place in the top of a steamer three quarters filled with hot water. Bring the water to the boil and cook the fish for 20 minutes.
2. Meanwhile, boil an egg for 10 minutes, and finely chop the parsley, gherkins and capers. When the egg is ready, peel it and chop finely.
3. Prepare a mayonnaise: put the 2 egg yolks in a bowl, add the mustard and beat in the oil a drop at a time with a whisk. When ready, add the lemon juice, salt, pepper, capers, gherkins, parsley and the chopped hard-boiled egg. Mix well and pour the sauce into a sauce boat.
4. When the fish is cooked, arrange the foil parcels on a serving dish and serve with the sauce.

This dish can be served cold with a salad.

Very often, fish is overcooked. Its delicate flesh gains very little by being cooked too long – it becomes hard, dry and tasteless. There is a small trick to check if the fish is cooked: pull out a bone near the head; if it comes out easily, the fish is ready.

Limande au Cidre ➤

Maquereaux Marinés à la Cannelle

Marinated Mackerel with Cinnamon

Serves 4. Preparation: 10 min
Marinade: 5 hr Cooking: 20 min
★

- ○ **1.2kg (2½ lb) small mackerel**
- ○ **½ litre (18 fl oz) dry white wine**
- ○ **4 medium-sized onions**
- ○ **2 cloves**
- ○ **1 small stick cinnamon**
- ○ **15ml (1 tbls) parsley, coarsely chopped**
- ○ **45ml (3 tbls) olive oil**
- ○ **2.5ml (½ tsp) peppercorns**
- ○ **salt**

1. Clean and rinse the fish under cold running water and dry on kitchen paper. Remove the heads. Peel and chop the onions. Place the mackerel in a salad bowl with the cloves, pepper, chopped onions, parsley and cinnamon. Season with salt and moisten with white wine. Cover and marinate for 5 hours, preferably in the fridge.
2. After 5 hours, peel and chop two more onions. Heat the oil in a saucepan and sauté the onions gently for approximately 5 minutes without browning.
3. Lift out and drain the mackerel and strain the marinade to remove the onions, parsley, pepper, cloves and cinnamon.
4. Place the fish on the bed of onions, add the marinade and enough water to cover. Cover and leave to cook gently for 15 minutes, without boiling.
5. Serve hot in the same dish.

Maquereaux au Vin Blanc

Mackerel in White Wine

Serves 4. Preparation: 20 min Cooking: 10 min
★

- ○ **1.2kg (2½ lb) small mackerel**
- ○ **½ litre (18 fl oz) dry white wine**
- ○ **¼ litre (9 fl oz) water**
- ○ **100ml (3½ fl oz) wine vinegar**
- ○ **2 medium-sized onions**
- ○ **2 carrots**
- ○ **1 lemon**
- ○ **1 bay leaf**
- ○ **1 sprig thyme**
- ○ **2 cloves**
- ○ **2.5ml (½ tsp) peppercorns**
- ○ **salt**

1. Peel and chop the onions and carrots. Place half of the vegetables at the bottom of a flameproof dish large enough to contain the fish. Rinse and cut the lemon in thin slices. Remove the pips.
2. Clean, rinse and dry the mackerel. Place on the vegetables, add the pepper, thyme, bay leaf and cloves. Season with salt, cover with the rest of the onions and carrots and add the wine and vinegar. The fish must be covered; add water if necessary.
3. Place the dish over a medium heat and when the liquid starts to simmer, cook for 5 minutes and then draw off the heat. Leave to cool in the dish and when it is completely cold, place in the fridge.

These mackerel can be kept in the fridge for 3 days: they are an excellent starter.

Mackerel is found everywhere; it is a migrating fish perfectly designed to swim fast, and can reach up to 60cm (2¼ ft) in length. Its flesh, similar to that of the tuna, is oily and savoury whether it is grilled, marinated, smoked, cooked in stock or in wine, hot or cold. Small mackerel, called liselettes, *are delicious, especially in a marinade.*

Unlike other fish, mackerel can be put into boiling stock; it makes the flesh firmer.

Never buy ready-prepared fillets; it may be the wrong fish. Buy it whole and ask your fishmonger to cut it into fillets.

Maquereaux aux Oignons

Serves 4. Preparation: 15 min Cooking: 30 min

Mackerel with Onions

★

○ **1.2kg (2½ lb) small mackerel**
○ **400ml (14 fl oz) dry white wine**
○ **3 onions, chopped finely**
○ **3 bay leaves**
○ **30ml (2 tbls) olive oil**
○ **salt and pepper**

1. Clean the fish, remove the heads and separate into fillets. Rinse and dry on kitchen paper. Crumble the bay leaves.
2. Place a layer of onions in a deep saucepan, add the fish, cover with the rest of the onions and sprinkle with bay leaves. Season with salt and pepper. Sprinkle with the oil and white wine. Cover, and allow to simmer for 30 minutes.
3. Serve hot in the same dish, with lemon quarters.

Merlans Farcis

Serves 4. Preparation: 20 min Cooking: 15 min

Stuffed Whiting

★★

○ **4 whiting, about 250g (9 oz) each**
○ **300g (10 oz) whiting fillets**
○ **50g (2 oz) white bread, with the crusts cut off**
○ **30ml (2 tbls) cream**
○ **1 egg**
○ **1 egg white**
○ **100g (4 oz) butter**
○ **30ml (2 tbls) breadcrumbs**
○ **the juice of 1 lemon**
○ **salt and pepper**
○ **nutmeg**

1. Scale, clean and rinse the fish under cold water. Remove the backbone without separating the fillets.
2. Put the whiting fillets, bread and cream in a blender. Put the mixture in a bowl and add the egg and the egg white. Season with salt, pepper and nutmeg, and stuff each whiting with the mixture. Secure with cocktail sticks.
3. Set the oven to 230°C (450°F; gas mark 8). Melt half of the butter in an ovenproof dish; lay in the fish, dust with breadcrumbs and add the rest of the butter. Bake for 15 minutes. Add the lemon juice 5 minutes before you take the fish out of the oven.

Serve hot with lemon quarters and a salad.

Merlans Poêlés en Persillade

Serves 4. Preparation: 10 min Cooking: 12 min

Fried Whiting with Parsley

○ **4 whiting, about 300g (11 oz) each**
○ **1 onion**
○ **2 cloves garlic**
○ **30ml (2 tbls) parsley, roughly chopped**
○ **100ml (3½ fl oz) dry white wine**
○ **50g (2 oz) butter**
○ **1 lemon**
○ **100ml (3½ fl oz) oil**
○ **salt and pepper**

1. Scale and clean the fish; remove the heads and rinse under cold water. Dry on kitchen paper. Peel the garlic and onions and chop finely.
2. Place the oil, onion and garlic, parsley and fish in a frying pan. Season with salt and pepper. Leave the whitings to cook gently for 3 minutes on each side, then add the wine. Allow to simmer for another 3-4 minutes, until the wine has reduced, then add the butter.
3. When the butter has melted, remove from heat, arrange the fish on a serving dish, pour over the cooking liquid and garnish with slices of lemon. Serve at once.

Serve this dish with baked tomatoes or salad.

Although not very exotic, boiled potatoes go very well with fried or poached fish. But all fresh vegetables are suitable: green beans, peas, grilled tomatoes, spinach, celery hearts, braised fennel, mushrooms and leeks fried in butter, boiled or steamed cauliflower. Try dried vegetables: dried white beans with angler, chick peas with tuna... Fresh pasta goes well with white fish cooked in sauce: brill or sole fillets, stewed cod, roast angler, etc.

Merlans au Sancerre
Whiting with White Wine

Serves 4. Preparation: 20 min Cooking: 20 min

★★

○ **4 whiting, about 300g (11 oz) each**
○ **200ml (7 fl oz) Sancerre**
○ **200g (7 oz) white bread**
○ **3 shallots**
○ **100g (4 oz) butter**
○ **salt and pepper**

1. Set the oven to 180°C (350°F; gas mark 4). Remove the bread crusts and cut into slices; bake in the oven for 10 minutes without letting it brown. When the bread is cold, grate finely to obtain nice white breadcrumbs. Put aside and set the oven to 230°C (450°F; gas mark 8).
2. With a sharp knife slit the fish along the back from head to tail. Cut the backbone from just below the head to the tail and remove it. Clean the fish through this opening and remove the black skin inside. Rinse under cold running water and dry on kitchen paper. Peel and chop the shallots finely.
3. Butter an ovenproof dish and cover the base with the shallots. Season with salt and pepper. Lay in the fish, opened flat, skin side down on the shallots. Season, dust each fish with breadcrumbs and dot with the remaining butter. Pour on the wine and bake for 12 to 15 minutes, until the breadcrumbs are golden brown.
4. When ready, arrange the fish on a serving dish, sprinkle with the cooking liquid and serve immediately.

Serve with lemon quarters and a salad. This recipe is also suitable for fillets of dab, dorado or cod.

Merlans aux Graines de Fenouil
Whiting with Fennel Seeds

Serves 4. Preparation and cooking: 35 min

★

○ **4 whiting, about 300g (11 oz) each**
○ **50g (2 oz) bacon**
○ **6 ripe tomatoes**
○ **2.5ml (½ tsp) fennel seeds**
○ **½ lemon**
○ **60ml (4 tbls) oil**
○ **salt and pepper**

1. Scale, clean and rinse the fish under cold water. Dry and sprinkle with lemon juice. Cut the bacon into small strips.
2. Scald the tomatoes in boiling water for 10 seconds, drain and refresh in cold water; peel, cut into halves and press to remove seeds. Crush to a pulp.
3. Fry the bacon in 30ml (2 tbls) of oil for 5 minutes, add the tomatoes and fennel seeds, season with salt and pepper and cook for a further 5 minutes.
4. Meanwhile, heat the remaining oil in another pan and sauté the whiting separately, 3 minutes on each side. Lift out, drain, and place in the pan with the bacon and tomatoes. Cover and leave to cook for 10 minutes.
5. When ready, arrange the fish on a serving dish, cover with the sauce and serve immediately.

In the nouvelle cuisine, *where the old principle of Brillat-Savarin that 'food must keep its taste' still holds, the idea of cooking white fish in stock has gradually been abandoned. It is now believed that they are best grilled in their scales, baked, poached or braised, or cooked* en papillotes. *This is true of bass, turbot, whiting, brill and sole.*

Merlans aux Épinards

Serves 4. Preparation and cooking: 35 min

Whiting with Spinach

★★

- ○ **4 whiting, about 300g (11 oz) each**
- ○ **100ml (3½ fl oz) water**
- ○ **100ml (3½ fl oz) dry white wine**
- ○ **2 cloves**
- ○ **4 mint leaves**
- ○ **250g (9 oz) spinach**
- ○ **salt and peppercorns**
- ○ **15ml (1 tbls) coarse salt**
- ○ **1 lemon**

For the sauce:
- ○ **40g (2 oz) butter**
- ○ **15ml (1 tbls) flour**
- ○ **200g (7 oz) cream**
- ○ **salt**
- ○ **nutmeg**

1. Scale, clean and rinse the fish under cold water. Dry on kitchen paper.
2. Place the fish in a saucepan, together with the cloves, mint and 6 peppercorns. Add the wine and water, bring to the boil and season with salt; cover and allow to simmer on low heat for 15 minutes.
3. Meanwhile, wash the spinach thoroughly, place in a saucepan without draining and season with salt. Cover tightly and place on a high heat for 4 minutes. Drain well and pass through the fine sieve of a moulinette (or vegetable mill). Reserve.
4. Lift out the fish and arrange in a deep serving dish.
5. Prepare the sauce: melt the butter, stir in the flour with a wooden spoon and add the cream. Season with salt and nutmeg. Let this sauce cook gently for 6 minutes, stirring continuously. Remove from the heat and add the spinach to the sauce, stirring well, then pour over the whiting.
6. Serve hot or cold with lemon quarters.

Merlans Farcis aux Champignons

Serves 4.
Preparation and cooking: 1 hr

Stuffed Whiting with Mushrooms

★★★

- ○ **4 whiting, about 250g (9 oz) each**
- ○ **250g (9 oz) button mushrooms**
- ○ **70g (3 oz) white bread, crusts removed**
- ○ **200ml (7 fl oz) dry white wine**
- ○ **2 anchovy fillets in oil**
- ○ **2 onions**
- ○ **15ml (1 tbls) parsley, coarsely chopped**
- ○ **15ml (1 tbls) basil, coarsely chopped**
- ○ **1 clove garlic**
- ○ **1 egg**
- ○ **80g (3½ oz) butter**
- ○ **salt and pepper**

1. Scale the whiting, slit along the front and clean through the opening; remove the backbone without separating the fillets. Rinse under cold water and dry. Remove stalks from the mushrooms, wash and chop finely.
2. Melt 20g (1 oz) of the butter in a frying pan and sauté the mushrooms over a high heat for 15 minutes, stirring frequently.
3. Meanwhile, prepare the stuffing: mix 45ml (3 tbls) of wine with the bread and mash with a fork; peel the onion and garlic, chop finely and add to the mixture; chop the anchovy fillets finely and add. Stir everything well together and add the basil, parsley, and egg. Season with salt and pepper.
4. When the mushrooms are cooked, mix into the stuffing and blend all well together.
5. Set the oven to 200°C (400°F; gas mark 6). Stuff the fish, reshape and stitch with white thread to prevent the stuffing from coming out during the cooking.
6. Butter an ovenproof dish and lay the fish in, sprinkle over the rest of the wine, dot with the remaining butter and bake for 25 minutes, basting frequently with the cooking liquid. Serve hot.

A purée of artichokes, celery or spinach goes very well with this dish.

To prepare raw fish the Japanese way: clean, cut into fillets and then in fine strips; served with soya sauce, grated black radish, thin slices of ginger, and green mustard with horseradish, it becomes the wonderful Japanese Sashimi, *which will convince anybody who tries it that raw fish is a feast.*

Merlu aux Oignons

Serves 4. Preparation and cooking: 55 min

Hake with Onions

★

- ○ **4 hake steaks, about 200g (7 oz) each**
- ○ **1kg (2¼ lb) onions**
- ○ **1 red pepper**
- ○ **100ml (3½ fl oz) vinegar**
- ○ **1 clove garlic**
- ○ **5ml (1 tsp) sugar**
- ○ **30ml (2 tbls) flour**
- ○ **120ml (8 tbls) ground nut oil**
- ○ **salt and pepper**
- ○ **nutmeg**

Serve with:
- ○ **1 hard-boiled egg**
- ○ **15ml (1 tbls) capers**
- ○ **10 green olives**

1. Peel and chop the onions finely. Wash the pepper, cut into quarters and remove the middle and the seeds. Cut into thin strips.
2. Heat 60ml (4 tbls) of oil and sauté the garlic, onions and pepper for 10 minutes. When the onions are golden brown, add the vinegar and sugar. Season with salt, pepper and nutmeg. Cover and cook gently for 20 minutes, stirring occasionally. Pour the mixture into a bowl and reserve.
3. Sprinkle the flour on a plate. Rinse and dry the fish steaks, dip in the flour and shake to remove excess.
4. Heat 60ml (4 tbls) of oil in a frying pan and fry the fish for 3 minutes on each side, until they are golden brown. Lift out, drain and arrange on a serving dish.
5. Pour the sauce over the steaks, allow to cool and add slices of hard-boiled egg, olives and capers.

Serve the same day or, even better, the following day.

Merlu Gratiné à la Tomme Fraîche

Serves 4. Preparation: 10 min
Cooking: 25 min Marinade: 30 min

Hake Gratin

★

- ○ **4 hake steaks, about 200g (7 oz) each**
- ○ **200g (7 oz) tomme de Savoie, if available, or another soft cheese**
- ○ **100g (4 oz) cream**
- ○ **250g (9 oz) ripe tomatoes**
- ○ **30ml (2 tbls) oil**
- ○ **juice of 1 lemon**
- ○ **salt and pepper**
- ○ **nutmeg**

1. Wash and dry the fish. Put in a dish, sprinkle with lemon juice, and leave to marinate for 30 minutes.
2. Meanwhile, scald the tomatoes in boiling water for 10 seconds, drain and refresh in cold water, then peel and cut into halves; press to remove seeds and crush to a pulp. Cut the cheese into thin slices.
3. Set the oven to 220°C (425°F; gas mark 7). Oil an ovenproof dish, arrange the fish in it and season with salt, pepper and nutmeg. Add the tomatoes, cover with slices of cheese and sprinkle the cream over. Bake for 25 minutes.
4. Serve hot in the same cooking dish.

Hake, called colin *in the Paris region, is often referred to as whiting in the South of France. Its firm white flesh, as lean as that of the sole, is very delicate. Although it can be found all year round, it is at its best in June.*

Small hake are delicious deep fried; large ones can be either baked or fried in butter. The largest, weighing up to 10kg (22 lb) are often sold in steaks and can be fried, or stewed with vegetables or tomatoes.

Hake is very fragile: it is fresh when its scales are still in place and when its three colours – black back, white front, and grey sides – are still visible. Its black eye should be very bright, like a pearl. If sold in steaks, its flesh should be milky white.

Merlu aux Poivrons

Serves 4. Preparation and cooking: 55 min

Hake with Peppers

★★

○ **4 hake steaks, about 200g (7 oz) each**
○ **3 red peppers**
○ **juice of 2 lemons**
○ **12 sage leaves**
○ **150ml (5 fl oz) oil**
○ **salt and pepper**

1. Light the grill. Wash and dry the peppers and place under the grill, turning frequently, until their skin turns black. Place the peppers in a saucepan, cover and leave on one side for 10 minutes.
2. Meanwhile, wash and dry the fish. Oil an ovenproof dish with 45ml (3 tbls) of oil and arrange the steaks in it. Sprinkle with lemon juice.
3. Set the oven to 200°C (400°F; gas mark 6). Peel the peppers, removing the black skin. Cut in halves and remove the seeds and centre. Cut into thin slices and place around the fish. Add the sage leaves and season with salt and pepper. Sprinkle over the rest of the oil and 15ml (1 tbls) of water.
4. Bake for 20 minutes and serve at once.

Suitable also for cod or tuna steaks.

Merlu à l'Orange

Serves 4. Preparation: 15 min Cooking: 20 min

Hake with Orange

★

○ **4 hake steaks, about 200g (7 oz) each**
○ **100ml (3½ fl oz) dry white wine**
○ **200g (7 oz) button mushrooms**
○ **3 oranges**
○ **45ml (3 tbls) breadcrumbs**
○ **50g (2 oz) butter**
○ **salt and pepper**

1. Wash the fish and dry on kitchen paper.
2. Remove the stalks of the mushrooms, wash and chop finely. Wash and slice the oranges without peeling.
3. Set the oven to 220°C (425°F; gas mark 7). Butter an ovenproof dish, lay in the fish steaks, sprinkle with white wine and place the mushrooms and oranges around. Sprinkle with breadcrumbs, dot with a few knobs of butter and season. Bake for 20 minutes and serve at once.

Morue au Lait et aux Pommes de Terre

Serves 4. Preparation: 10 min
Cooking: 35 min

Salt Cod with Milk and Potatoes

★

○ **600g (1½ lb) salt cod, soaked in water**
○ **500g (1 lb) potatoes**
○ **1 litre (2 pints) milk**
○ **100g (4 oz) cream**
○ **40g (1¾ oz) butter**
○ **30ml (2 tbls) parsley, coarsely chopped**
○ **salt and pepper**

1. Remove the skin and bones and cut the salt cod into small cubes. Peel and slice the potatoes.
2. Butter a saucepan; put in the fish and potatoes. Cover with the milk and cream, season with pepper and a little salt. Bring to the boil, reduce the heat and allow to cook for 30 minutes without the lid.
3. When ready, place on a serving dish, sprinkle with parsley and serve immediately.

The merou *is the common name for a lovely fish, found in the Mediterranean and South Atlantic coastal waters, which can only be fished with a harpoon. Its delicate white flesh is like shellfish. Delicious in* bouillabaisse, *it has no equal when served cold.*

Merlu aux Poivrons ▶

Boulettes de Morue au Basilic

Salt Cod Balls with Basil

Serves 4. Preparation: 20 min
Cooking: 40 min
★★

- ○ 500g (1 lb) salt cod, soaked in water
- ○ 2 eggs
- ○ 50g (2 oz) white bread
- ○ 100ml (3½ fl oz) warm milk
- ○ 15ml (1 tbls) grated Parmesan
- ○ 100g (4 oz) breadcrumbs
- ○ oil for frying
- ○ salt and pepper
- ○ nutmeg

For the sauce:
- ○ 1 400g (14 oz) tin peeled tomatoes
- ○ 30g (1 oz) butter
- ○ 6 basil leaves
- ○ 1 clove garlic, unpeeled
- ○ salt

1. Remove the skin and bones and chop the salt cod finely. Place the bread in the warm milk, allow to swell, then crumble with a fork.
2. Mix the fish with the eggs, season with salt, pepper and nutmeg and add the Parmesan. Drain the bread and stir into the mixture. Work it together with your hand and shape into small balls the size of an egg. Dip in breadcrumbs.
3. Prepare the sauce: cut the peeled tomatoes in halves and remove the seeds. Place in a saucepan with their juice, the butter, unpeeled clove of garlic and basil leaves. Season with salt. Cover and allow to simmer for 20 minutes.
4. Meanwhile, heat the oil in a frying pan and fry the fish balls for approximately 5 minutes until golden brown. Drain on kitchen paper.
5. When the sauce is ready, add the fish balls and allow to cook gently for another 15 minutes.

Serve hot with warm white beans, chickpeas or pilau rice.

Morue Gratinée à la Sauce Tomate

Salt Cod Gratin with Tomato Sauce

Serves 4.
Preparation and cooking: 1 hr
★★

- ○ 800g (1¾ lb) salt cod, soaked in water
- ○ 60ml (4 tbls) flour
- ○ 1 egg
- ○ 15ml (1 tbls) olive oil
- ○ ½ lemon
- ○ 30ml (2 tbls) breadcrumbs
- ○ oil for frying
- ○ salt

For the sauce:
- ○ 1 400g (14 oz) tin peeled tomatoes
- ○ 1 clove garlic, finely chopped
- ○ 100g (4 oz) green olives, stoned
- ○ 3 anchovy fillets
- ○ 30ml (2 tbls) parsley, roughly chopped
- ○ 90ml (6 tbls) olive oil
- ○ salt and pepper

1. Beat the egg as for an omelette with the 15ml (1 tbls) of olive oil. Season with salt. Grate the lemon peel and mix with the breadcrumbs. Sprinkle a plate with the flour.
2. Remove the skin and bones and cut the salt cod into large cubes. Dip the fish first in the flour, then in the egg and lastly in the seasoned breadcrumbs.
3. Heat the oil in a frying pan and fry the cubes of fish for 5 minutes on each side, drain on kitchen paper.
4. Prepare the sauce: cut the tomatoes in halves and remove the seeds. Crush to a pulp and keep the juice. Fry the garlic until pale golden and add the tomatoes and juice. Season with salt and pepper. Leave to cook over a high heat for 10 minutes.
5. Set the oven to 220°C (425°F; gas mark 7). Chop the anchovy fillets finely and oil an ovenproof dish. Put a layer of tomatoes at the bottom, arrange the fish on top and cover with the sauce. Sprinkle with green olives, anchovy fillets and chopped parsley. Bake for 10 minutes and serve hot.

You may add capers to the sauce and serve this dish with hot toast and a green salad.

Morue Gratinée aux Oignons
Salt Cod Gratin with Onions

Serves 4. Preparation and cooking: 45 min

- ○ **800g (2 lb) salt cod, soaked**
- ○ **200ml (7 fl oz) dry white wine**
- ○ **6 onions**
- ○ **30g (1 oz) butter**
- ○ **30ml (2 tbls) oil**
- ○ **2 bay leaves**
- ○ **1 sprig thyme**
- ○ **70g (3 oz) Gruyère, grated**
- ○ **salt and pepper**

1. Cut the salt cod into 5cm (2 inch) pieces and put in a saucepan. Add the thyme and bay leaves, cover with water and bring to the boil. Reduce the heat and allow to simmer for 10 minutes. Drain and leave to cool.
2. Meanwhile, peel and chop the onions finely. Fry gently in oil and butter for 10 minutes and add the wine. Season with salt and pepper and boil until the wine has reduced.
3. Set the oven to 220°C (425°F; gas mark 7). Remove the skin and bones and place the fish in an ovenproof dish. Cover with the onions, sprinkle with grated cheese and a few knobs of butter. Bake for 5 minutes and serve hot in the same dish.

You can accompany this fish dish with small fried croûtons.

Morue Gratinée au Lait
Salt Cod Gratin with Milk

Serves 4. Preparation and cooking: 50 min

★★

- ○ **800g (2 lb) salt cod, soaked**
- ○ **80g (3 oz) butter**
- ○ **45ml (3 tbls) oil**
- ○ **3 onions, finely chopped**
- ○ **250ml (½ pint) milk**
- ○ **25g (1 oz) flour**
- ○ **50g (2 oz) Gruyère (or other mild cheese), grated**
- ○ **salt and pepper**
- ○ **nutmeg**

1. Cut the salt cod into 3 inch pieces and put in a saucepan with enough cold water to cover the fish. Bring to the boil, reduce the heat and cook gently for 10 minutes.
2. Meanwhile, fry the onions in oil and 50g (2 oz) of butter until they are pale yellow, stir in the flour and add the milk slowly, stirring continuously. Season with salt, pepper and nutmeg. Blend until smooth and remove from the heat.
3. When the fish has cooked for 10 minutes, drain, remove the skin and bones and flake. Set the oven to 220°C (425°F; gas mark 7).
4. Butter an ovenproof dish with half of the remaining butter and pour on half of the sauce. Arrange the fish in the dish and cover with the rest of the sauce. Sprinkle the cheese over and dot with butter. Bake for 20 minutes, until golden brown.
5. Serve hot in the same dish.

Serve this dish with leaf spinach or steamed cauliflower.

Soak the salt cod the day before to remove salt: cut into 5cm (2 inch) pieces, wash in cold running water to remove salt grains and place in a large bowl, skin side up. Change the water as often as possible. To make it easier, put the fish in a colander and the colander in a large bowl.

Cooking is very simple: cover the fish with cold water and put on the heat. As soon as the water begins to tremble, skim the top, remove from the heat – or put the heat very low – and poach for 8 to 12 minutes, depending on the size of the pieces of fish. Salt cod should never be boiled as it becomes hard, yellow and stringy. Cooked properly, it can be prepared in many interesting ways.

Aioli de Morue

Salt Cod Aioli

Serves 6. Preparation and cooking: 50 min

★★

- ○ **1.2kg (2½ lb) salt cod, soaked**
- ○ **6 potatoes**
- ○ **6 hard-boiled eggs**
- ○ **12 carrots**
- ○ **12 turnips**
- ○ **6 leeks**
- ○ **250g (9 oz) green beans**
- ○ **6 tomatoes**
- ○ **4 cloves garlic**
- ○ **2 egg yolks**
- ○ **300ml (10 fl oz) olive oil**
- ○ **salt**

1. Wash and peel the potatoes and place in a saucepan with enough water to cover them. Bring to the boil and cook for approximately 15 minutes, testing with a sharp knife.
2. Peel and wash the carrots, turnips, leeks and green beans. Cut the salt fish into 5cm (2 inch) pieces. Place the vegetables in salted boiled water (first the carrots and leeks and 5 minutes later the turnips and green beans) and cook for 20 minutes.
3. Put the salt fish in a separate saucepan with enough cold water to cover, bring to the boil gently and allow to simmer for 8 minutes. Then remove from the heat and cover the pan.
4. Meanwhile, prepare the aioli: peel and chop the garlic finely, crush with salt in a mortar and add the egg yolks. Stir in the oil with a whisk as for a mayonnaise – you can use an electric beater.
5. When the vegetables are cooked, remove with a slotted spoon and arrange on a serving dish. Add the salt fish, cover with foil and keep warm in a slow oven.
6. Chop the hard-boiled eggs into quarters. Wash the tomatoes and cut into four pieces. Add to the fish dish, and serve with the sauce separately.

This dish with aioli (name of both sauce and the recipe) can be prepared with other fish: sea-bass, hake, whiting etc.

Other seasonal vegetables can be added: artichoke hearts, asparagus, broad beans, cauliflower, fennel, celery etc.

Shellfish is also suitable: for example, winkles boiled for 15 minutes in salted water.

Brandade de Morue

Brandade of Salt Cod

Serves 4. Preparation and cooking: 45 min

★★

- ○ **1kg (2¼ lb) salt cod, soaked**
- ○ **250ml (½ pint) warm milk**
- ○ **250ml (9 fl oz) olive oil**
- ○ **salt and nutmeg**

Optional:
- ○ **1 clove garlic, peeled**

1. Cut the salt cod into pieces and place in a saucepan with enough cold water to cover. Bring to the boil and allow to simmer for 10 minutes. Drain and leave to cool. Remove the skin and bones and flake with a fork.
2. Heat 100ml (3½ fl oz) of oil in another saucepan, add the fish and beat the mixture vigorously with a wooden spoon until it is reduced to a smooth paste. Then, a little at a time, add the rest of the oil and the milk, alternating each spoonful: after 20 minutes you should have a fine purée which comes away from the side of the pan. Crush the garlic and add the juice to the mixture. Season with salt and nutmeg.

Serve very hot with black olives and croûtons fried in olive oil and rubbed with garlic; it is delicious.

Gratin de Morue à l'Origan

Serves 4. Preparation and cooking: 1 hr 15 min

Salt Cod Gratin with Oregano

★ ★

- ○ **800g (2 lb) salt cod, soaked**
- ○ **500g (1 lb) ripe tomatoes**
- ○ **3 medium-sized potatoes**
- ○ **2 red or green peppers**
- ○ **1 onion, finely chopped**
- ○ **1 clove garlic**
- ○ **30ml (2 tbls) parsley, coarsely chopped**
- ○ **2.5ml (½ tsp) oregano**
- ○ **30ml (2 tbls) breadcrumbs**
- ○ **90ml (6 tbls) oil**
- ○ **salt and pepper**

1. Remove the skin and bones and cut the salt cod into 5cm (2 inch) pieces. Wash the peppers and cut into four, lengthwise. Remove the seeds and middle and slice each quarter. Peel the potatoes and slice into thin rounds.
2. Heat 30ml (2 tbls) of oil in a frying pan and sauté the onion gently for 5 minutes, then add the peppers and cook slowly for 10 minutes over low heat. Season with salt and pepper.
3. Scald the tomatoes (except for two) in boiling water for 10 seconds, drain and refresh in cold water; peel, cut into halves, remove the seeds and crush to a pulp.
4. Set the oven to 200°C (400°F; gas mark 6). Peel and chop the garlic finely. Slice the two remaining tomatoes.
5. Oil an ovenproof dish with 30ml (2 tbls) of oil. Put in first the crushed tomatoes, then the potatoes and sprinkle with the garlic and parsley. Pour over the onion and pepper mixture and add the salt cod. Cover with slices of tomato and season.
6. Dust with oregano, the rest of the garlic, parsley and breadcrumbs. Sprinkle with the oil and bake for 30 minutes. Serve hot.

Morue aux Raisins de Corinthe

Serves 4. Preparation: 15 min
Cooking: 30 min

Salt Cod with Currants

★

- ○ **800g (2 lb) salt cod, soaked**
- ○ **50g (2 oz) currants**
- ○ **2 onions, finely chopped**
- ○ **15ml (1 tbls) tomato purée**
- ○ **30ml (2 tbls) flour**
- ○ **60ml (4 tbls) oil**
- ○ **salt**

1. Soak the currants in warm water.
2. Remove the skin and bones and cut the salt cod into 8cm (3 inch) pieces. Dip in flour and shake to remove excess.
3. Heat the oil in a frying pan and sauté the onions gently for 5 minutes. Add the salt cod and sauté gently for 2 minutes on each side. Add the tomato purée diluted in 200ml (7 fl oz) water and bring to the boil. Drain the currants and place in the frying pan. Season with salt and simmer for 15 minutes, without boiling.
4. When ready, arrange the salt cod on a serving dish, pour the sauce over and serve immediately.

When using a court-bouillon *you must ensure that it is cold before immersing and cooking the fish. In this way the fish can cook gradually without disintegrating.*

Moreover, it should not be allowed to boil, but only simmer. Count 25 minutes for a 3 lb fish to be served hot. If the fish is to be served cold, place it in cold stock; when it starts to boil remove from the heat, cover and allow the fish to cool in the stock.

Mulet Rôti aux Aromates

Serves 4. Preparation: 15 min Cooking: 30 min

Roast Grey Mullet with Herbs

★

- ○ 1.2kg (2½ lb) grey mullet
- ○ 1 small pimento
- ○ 2 cloves garlic
- ○ 5ml (1 tsp) rosemary
- ○ 2.5ml (½ tsp) thyme
- ○ 2.5ml (½ tsp) fennel seeds
- ○ 30ml (2 tbls) breadcrumbs
- ○ 100ml (3½ fl oz) olive oil
- ○ juice of 1 lemon
- ○ salt and pepper

1. Scale, clean and wash the mullet and dry on kitchen paper. Season with salt and pepper inside and out. Oil an ovenproof dish with 15ml (1 tbls) of oil, lay in the fish and sprinkle with lemon juice.
2. Set the oven to 200°C (400°F; gas mark 6). Prepare the seasoned oil: peel and crush the garlic in a mortar with 2.5ml (½ tsp) salt, the pimento, rosemary, fennel and thyme; mix well with the remaining oil.
3. Coat the fish with this oil, dust with breadcrumbs and bake for 30 minutes, basting from time to time with the cooking juices. Serve very hot.

Muge en Raïto

Serves 3-4. Preparation and cooking: 50 min

Grey Mullet Provençal-Style

★ ★

- ○ 1.2kg (2½ lb) grey mullet
- ○ 30ml (2 tbls) flour
- ○ 100ml (3½ fl oz) peanut oil

For the sauce:
- ○ 3 ripe tomatoes or 15ml (1 tbls) tomato purée
- ○ 2 onions
- ○ 2 cloves garlic
- ○ 1 bouquet garni: bay leaf, 5 sprigs parsley
- ○ 200ml (7 fl oz) red wine
- ○ 100ml (3½ fl oz) boiling water
- ○ 30ml (2 tbls) capers
- ○ 24 black olives
- ○ 45ml (3 tbls) olive oil
- ○ salt and pepper

1. Scale and clean the mullet and cut into 5cm (2 inch) thick slices. Dip the fish in flour and shake to remove excess. Reserve.
2. Prepare the sauce: scald the tomatoes for 10 seconds in boiling water, drain and refresh in cold water. Peel, cut in halves and remove the seeds. Crush to a pulp. Peel the onions and garlic and chop finely.
3. Heat the olive oil in a saucepan, sauté the onions for 5 minutes on a low heat, then add the wine, turn up the heat and reduce for 5 minutes. Add the boiling water, crushed tomatoes, chopped garlic and bouquet garni and season with salt and pepper. Reduce the heat and leave to cook gently for 10 minutes, stirring from time to time with a wooden spoon.
4. Meanwhile, heat the peanut oil in a frying pan and fry the slices of fish for 2 minutes on each side until golden, then lift out and drain on kitchen paper.
5. When the sauce has cooked for 10 minutes, add the fish, capers and olives and allow to simmer for a further 10 minutes. Remove the bouquet garni.
6. Place the slices of mullet on a serving dish, coat with the sauce and serve at once.

Croûtons fried in oil or butter can accompany this recipe.

Mullet Provencal-style is the main course of the traditional meal served in the region of Arles on Christmas Eve, before the midnight mass. Other firm-fleshed fish can be prepared in the same way: bass, brill, salt cod or cod. It can be either fried, baked or boiled in stock, but is invariably left to simmer for 10 minutes in the sauce before serving.

Mulets aux Fines Herbes

Serves 4. Preparation: 20 min Cooking: 15 min

Grey Mullet with Herbs

★

○ **4 grey mullet, about 300g (11 oz) each**
○ **100ml (3½ fl oz) oil**
○ **100ml (3½ fl oz) dry white wine**
○ **juice of 1 lemon**
○ **1 small pimento**
○ **3 anchovy fillets, in oil**
○ **1 basil leaf**
○ **6 sage leaves**
○ **20 sprigs parsley**
○ **1 bay leaf (fresh)**
○ **15ml (1 tbls) vinegar**
○ **salt and pepper**

1. Scale, clean and wash the mullet and dry on kitchen paper. Arrange in an ovenproof dish and season with salt and pepper.
2. Beat together the oil and lemon juice and reserve. Set the oven to 220°C (425°F; gas mark 7).
3. Finely chop the anchovies, pimento, basil, sage, parsley and bay leaf. Add the vinegar and 15ml (1 tbls) of the oil-lemon mixture. Coat the fish with this thick paste and sprinkle with the rest of the oil-lemon mixture and white wine.
4. Bake for 15 minutes and serve hot.

Serve with tomatoes 'Provençal-style' or a mixed salad: endive and fennel, for instance.

Mulet à la Crème et aux Poivrons

Serves 4. Preparation: 20 min Cooking: 30 min

Grey Mullet with Cream and Peppers

★

○ **1 mullet, 1.2kg (2½ lb)**
○ **juice of 1 lemon**
○ **50g (2 oz) bacon**
○ **2 peppers**
○ **50g (2 oz) butter**
○ **1 large onion**
○ **4 ripe tomatoes**
○ **100g (4 oz) cream**
○ **15ml (1 tbls) mustard, (Dijon preferably)**
○ **salt**

1. Scale, clean and wash the mullet under cold running water and dry on kitchen paper. Sprinkle with lemon juice and season with salt both inside and out.
2. Set the oven to 220°C (425°F; gas mark 7). Cut the bacon into small pieces. Wash the peppers, remove the seeds, chop into quarters, then slice each quarter finely. Peel the onion and chop finely. Scald the tomatoes for 10 seconds in boiling water, drain and refresh in cold water. Peel, cut into halves and press to remove the seeds. Crush to a pulp with a fork.
3. Butter an ovenproof dish with 20g (¾ oz) of the butter and lay in the mullet. Cover with the bacon and half of the peppers and surround with the rest of the peppers, onion and tomatoes. Melt the remaining butter and pour over the fish. Bake for 20 minutes, basting from time to time with the cooking juices.
4. Meanwhile, mix the cream and mustard and season with salt. Pour this sauce over the fish and cook for a further 10 minutes. Serve hot.

Serve with pilau rice.

The mostelle, a fish of the gade family, is found mainly in the Mediterranean. This fish is very delicately flavoured and must be eaten fresh on the spot, as it does not travel well.

The best way to prepare it is to slit it open along the back, remove the backbone, season with salt and dot with butter. Bake in the oven, basting frequently. Serve with a squeeze of lemon.

Filets de Perche à la Sauge

Perch Fillets with Sage

Serves 4. Preparation: 5 min Cooking: 15 min

★

- ○ **8 perch fillets**
- ○ **250g (9 oz) cream**
- ○ **10 sage leaves (fresh)**
- ○ **40g (1¼ oz) butter**
- ○ **salt and white pepper**

1. Wash and dry the fillets.
2. Set the oven to 220°C (425°F; gas mark 7). Pour the cream into a saucepan and bring to the boil.
3. Butter an ovenproof dish with 20g (¾ oz) of butter, cover the base with sage leaves, place the fillets on top and season with salt and pepper. Pour over the cream, dot with butter and bake for 15 minutes.
4. When the fillets are ready, serve at once.

Braised celery hearts or steamed potatoes are suitable with this dish.

Perches à la Crème et aux Champignons

Perch with Cream and Mushrooms

Serves 4.
Preparation and cooking: 50 min
★ ★

- ○ **1.2kg (2½ lb) perch**
- ○ **300g (10 oz) button mushrooms**
- ○ **30g (1¼ oz) butter**
- ○ **30ml (2 tbls) oil**
- ○ **250ml (9 fl oz) dry white wine**
- ○ **200g (7 oz) cream**
- ○ **2 shallots**
- ○ **15ml (1 tbls) parsley, coarsely chopped**
- ○ **salt and pepper**

1. Scale, clean and wash the fish under cold running water and dry.
2. Remove the stalks of the mushrooms, wash and chop finely. Peel the shallots and chop finely.
3. Heat the oil in a frying pan, and add the butter and mushrooms. Dust with half of the parsley and cook for 10 minutes on a high heat, stirring with a wooden spoon.
4. Set the oven to 220°C (425°F; gas mark 7). Lay the shallots at the bottom of an ovenproof dish, add the mushrooms, the remaining parsley and the fish, sprinkle with wine and season with salt and pepper.
5. Bake for 20 minutes, basting frequently with the cooking juices. When cooked, pour the cream over the fish and allow to cook for a further 5 minutes.
6. Serve immediately.

Perch can be found in small or large rivers. Small ones can be deep fried whereas the large ones are cut into fillets or served in batter. If not scaled immediately, perch must be skinned like an eel.

The brown hog-fish, called small because it is not longer than 30cm (12 inches), is exquisite in fish soup and indispensable in bouillabaise. It can be found among seaweed-covered rocks in the Mediterranean and Gulf of Gascony regions – its colours of brown, pink and grey often cause it to be mistaken for weed. Its cousin the red hog-fish is larger and less appreciated.

There is a third type, called the dorado hog-fish, which can be found in the rocky depths of the North Atlantic and can weigh up to 2kg (4½ lb). It is served in fillets which are fried or poached because its flesh is very oily.

Raie au Beurre Noir

Serves 4. Preparation and cooking: 45 min

Skate with Black Butter

★

○ **1kg (2½ lb) skate, cut in 4 pieces**
○ **180g (6 oz) butter**
○ **30ml (2 tbls) parsley, coarsely chopped**
○ **45ml (3 tbls) capers**
○ **30ml (2 tbls) wine vinegar**

For the court-bouillon:
○ **100ml (3½ fl oz) vinegar**
○ **1 onion**
○ **1 carrot**
○ **1 bouquet garni, consisting of: bay leaf, sprig thyme, 5 sprigs parsley**
○ **6 peppercorns**
○ **15ml (1 tbls) coarse salt**

1. Remove the skin and wash the skate under running water. Peel the onion and carrot and chop finely.
2. Place the pieces of skate in a large saucepan, cover with cold water, and add the carrot, onion, bouquet garni, peppercorns, salt and vinegar. Put on a low heat; the minute it comes to the boil, reduce the heat and barely simmer for 20 minutes – it must not boil. Skim the top when it first begins to boil.
3. After 20 minutes drain the skate and arrange the pieces on a serving dish; sprinkle with capers and parsley and keep warm.
4. Melt the butter in a frying pan and heat until it turns a caramel colour (not black, in spite of the name!), and pour over the fish. Add the wine vinegar to the pan, heat for 2 seconds, then pour it over the fish.

Serve hot on its own or with small steamed potatoes.

Rougets en Papillotes

Serves 4. Preparation: 15 min Cooking: 12 min

Red Mullet in Foil

★

○ **8 red mullet, about 180g (6 oz) each**
○ **4 stems fresh fennel (or rosemary, basil or fresh savory)**
○ **30ml (2 tbls) olive oil**
○ **salt and pepper**
○ **foil**

1. Scale and wash the fish under cold running water. Clean through the gills, remove the liver and replace with a few fennel leaves. Dry on kitchen paper.
2. Set the oven to 220°C (425°F; gas mark 7). Cut 8 rectangles of aluminium foil, each large enough to contain a fish.
3. Oil each red mullet and place in the foil with salt, pepper and fennel; close each packet by twisting both ends.
4. Place the packets on a baking sheet and bake for 12 minutes.

Serve the red mullets in their foil with lemon quarters and anchovy butter prepared as follows: mix 15ml (1 tbls) of anchovy paste with 100g (4 oz) soft butter and add a few drops of garlic juice.

Char is a highly sought after delicacy. It can be prepared like salmon when small and like trout when larger, and is found in the deep lakes and rivers of Switzerland, the Auvergne and the Pyrenees.

There are many types of skate, but the best can be recognised by the large bony marks under the skin. As your fishmonger will only sell you the wings, you will have to trust him!

The small skate is best fried. First clean and skin it (having scalded it beforehand), cut off the head and keep the liver, much prized by connoisseurs.

The best recipe for skate is with beurre noir, *but it is worth trying others: with white sauce, or baked with a cheese* béchamel *on a bed of thinly sliced potato rounds.*

Rougets en Sauce Tomate

Red Mullet with Tomato Sauce

Serves 4. Preparation: 15 min Cooking: 35 min

★★

○ **8 medium-sized red mullet**
○ **30ml (2 tbls) flour**
○ **oil for frying**

For the sauce:
○ **500g (1 lb) ripe tomatoes**
○ **45ml (3 tbls) oil**
○ **1 clove garlic**
○ **1 onion**
○ **1 bouquet garni: thyme, basil, bay leaf**
○ **15ml (1 tbls) parsley, coarsely chopped**
○ **100ml (3½ fl oz) dry white wine**
○ **salt**

1. Scale, clean and wash the mullet under cold running water and dry. Dip in flour.
2. Peel the garlic and onion and chop finely. Tie up the bouquet garni. Scald the tomatoes for 10 seconds in boiling water, drain and refresh in cold water; peel, cut into halves and press to remove seeds. Crush to a pulp with a fork and reserve.
3. Fry the red mullet in oil for 2 minutes on each side then lift out and drain on kitchen paper. Pour away the frying oil and wipe the frying pan clean.
4. Heat the 45ml (3 tbls) of oil in the frying pan and gently sauté the garlic and onion for about 5 minutes. Add the tomatoes, bouquet garni, white wine and chopped parsley. Season with salt and bring to the boil. Allow to simmer for 20 minutes, stirring from time to time with a wooden spoon.
5. After 20 minutes add the red mullet to the sauce and leave to cook for a further 2 minutes on each side. Serve hot or cold.

Rougets à l'Orientale

Red Mullet Oriental-Style

Serves 4. Preparation: 15 min
Cooking: 10 min, 12 hr in advance

★

○ **8 small mullet**
○ **300ml (10 fl oz) dry white wine**
○ **4 sprigs parsley**
○ **1 fennel stem**
○ **1 sprig thyme**
○ **1 bay leaf**
○ **12 coriander seeds**
○ **6 peppercorns**
○ **2 cloves**
○ **2 pinches of saffron**
○ **15ml (1 tbls) oil**
○ **1 lemon**
○ **salt**

1. Scale and wash the red mullet but do not gut them. Dry on kitchen paper and season with salt.
2. Oil a big flameproof dish and lay the fish in side by side.
3. Pour the white wine over the fish and add water to cover if necessary. Add the parsley, fennel, thyme, bay leaf, coriander, saffron, cloves and peppercorns. Season with a little salt.
4. Place the dish over a low heat. The minute it begins to boil lower the heat and allow to simmer for 5 minutes. Remove from the heat.
5. Cut the lemon in thin slices and garnish the dish. Allow to cool for at least 12 hours before serving.

This can be kept in the fridge without ruining its flavour, and it makes a delicious first course. In winter, add thin slices of oranges with the lemon; in summer, add roughly chopped tomatoes to the red mullet before pouring over the wine.

There are two types of red mullet: rougets-barbets *and* surmulets. *Both are small, no more than 30cm (12 inches) in length, with two long barbels on the lower jaw; the brown-green back and silvery flanks become red when taken out of the water. The* surmulets *are rock mullets whereas the others inhabit the muddy bottom of the sea. They are best fried without being cleaned or scaled and try the liver: it is delicious.*

Roussette au Riz Doré

Serves 4. Preparation and cooking: 30 min

Dogfish with Golden Rice

★★

○ **1kg (2¼ lb) dogfish**
○ **250g (9 oz) long-grain rice**
○ **30g (1¼ oz) butter**
○ **3 pinches of saffron**
○ **salt**

For the sauce:
○ **30ml (2 tbls) tomato purée**
○ **3 chopped shallots**
○ **250ml (9 fl oz) dry white wine**
○ **100ml (3½ fl oz) madeira wine**
○ **30ml (2 tbls) brandy**
○ **125g (4 oz) cream**
○ **5ml (1 tsp) tarragon, coarsely chopped**
○ **1 small pimento**
○ **1 bouquet garni: bay leaf, 5 sprigs parsley**
○ **60ml (4 tbls) oil**
○ **salt and pepper**

1. Boil some water in a saucepan. Rinse and drain the rice and place in boiling water with the saffron. Leave to cook gently for 18 minutes. Test the rice after 15 minutes.
2. Meanwhile, wash the fish under cold water, cut into 5cm (2 inch) pieces and dry on kitchen paper. Sauté the fish in oil for 2 minutes on each side, and when golden add the tomato purée diluted in white wine, and the madeira, shallot, crushed pimento and bouquet garni. Season with salt and pepper. Leave to cook gently for 15 minutes.
3. Set the oven to 180°C (350°F; gas mark 4). When the rice is cooked, drain, add the butter and put in an ovenproof dish. Place in the oven to dry while preparing the sauce.
4. When the sauce has cooked for 15 minutes add the brandy, cream and chopped tarragon. Mix well and leave to cook for another 5 minutes and remove the bouquet garni.
5. Arrange the fish on a serving dish, coat with the sauce and serve with the rice separately.

Roussette à la Rouille

Serves 4. Preparation and cooking: 1 hr

Dogfish with Saffron Sauce

★★

○ **1kg (2¼ lb) dogfish**

For the court-bouillon:
○ **1 carrot**
○ **1 chopped onion**
○ **1 clove**
○ **1 sprig thyme**
○ **1 bay leaf**
○ **100ml (3½ fl oz) vinegar**
○ **15ml (1 tbls) coarse salt**
○ **6 peppercorns**

For the sauce:
○ **50g (2 oz) white bread**
○ **1 egg yolk**
○ **2 cloves garlic**
○ **2 small pimentos**
○ **2 pinches of saffron**
○ **200ml (7 fl oz) olive oil**
○ **salt**

1. Wash the fish and cut into 5cm (2 inch) pieces. Dry on kitchen paper. Peel and slice the carrot.
2. Prepare the stock: put the onion, carrot, thyme, bay leaf, cloves, peppercorns in a saucepan together with 1½ litres (3 pints) of water and the vinegar. Bring to the boil, season with salt, reduce the heat and allow to simmer for 20 minutes. Leave to cool.
3. When the stock is cold, add the fish and bring to the boil. At the first bubble, reduce the heat and allow to simmer for 5 minutes. Leave the fish to cool in the stock.
4. Prepare the sauce: peel the garlic. Place the bread in a mortar, add 30ml (2 tbls) of stock, the garlic and pimentos and grind finely together. Add the saffron and egg yolk, mix together, and stir in the oil drop by drop as for mayonnaise. Season lightly with salt.
5. When the fish is cold, arrange it on a serving dish and serve with the sauce separately.

As this sauce is rather strong, you might prefer an aioli or tartare sauce: mayonnaise with chives, capers and chopped gherkins.

Cod is also suitable for this recipe.

Saint-Pierre aux Poireaux

Serves 4. Preparation: 15 min Cooking: 30 min

John Dory with Leeks

★★

- ○ **2 John Dorys, about 800g (2 lb) each**
- ○ **8 leeks**
- ○ **200g (7 oz) cream**
- ○ **50g (2 oz) butter**
- ○ **100ml (3½ fl oz) white vermouth**
- ○ **salt and pepper**

1. Clean and skin the fish and separate into fillets. Wash under cold running water and dry on kitchen paper.
2. Discard the green parts of the leeks. Wash and slice into thin rounds.
3. Melt the butter in a saucepan and gently sauté the leeks for 10 minutes. Season with salt and pepper, sprinkle with the vermouth and let it evaporate.
4. Pour on the cream and when it starts to bubble, add the fillets. Leave to cook gently for 10 minutes, turning them halfway through.
5. Lift out the fillets and arrange on a serving dish. Keep warm.
6. Reduce the sauce for 2 minutes over a high heat and pour over the fish. Serve at once.

Fillets of sole, turbot or brill can be prepared in the same way.

Sandre au Beurre Blanc

Serves 4. Preparation and cooking: 30 min

Pike-Perch with Butter Sauce

★★★

- ○ **1 pike-perch, about 1.5kg (3¼ lb)**
- ○ **250g (9 oz) slightly salted butter**
- ○ **4 shallots**
- ○ **100ml (3½ fl oz) white wine vinegar**
- ○ **150ml (5 fl oz) white wine**
- ○ **white pepper**

1. Ask your fishmonger to clean the fish through the gills. Do not scale. Light the grill.
2. When the grill is hot enough, grill the fish for 5 minutes on each side. Set the oven at 200°C (400°F; gas mark 6) and bake the pike-perch for 15 minutes.
3. Meanwhile, prepare the butter sauce: peel and finely chop the shallots. Put them in a heavy-based saucepan and add the vinegar and white wine.
4. Place the saucepan on a medium heat and allow to reduce until there is 15ml (1 tbls) of liquid left and the sauce has become syrupy. Remove from the heat. Cut the butter into cubes.
5. Away from the heat, add a nut of butter, whisking vigorously, and then beat in the rest of the butter, one nut after the other, keeping the saucepan just on a low heat. It is easier if you stand the saucepan on an asbestos sheet over a low heat: your sauce will be smooth, warm and velvety.
6. When the sauce is ready, add the freshly ground white pepper and pour into a sauce boat.
7. Arrange the pike-perch on a serving dish and serve the sauce separately.

Fish cooked in this way will keep its flavour. The skin comes off easily and the flesh is soft, succulent and delicious. Salmon or bass can be prepared in the same way.

Sardines Rôties Farcies

Serves 6. Preparation: 45 min Cooking: 15 min

Stuffed Sardines in the Oven

★★

○ **1.5kg (3¼ lb) sardines**
○ **60ml (4 tbls) breadcrumbs**
○ **6 bay leaves**
○ **90ml (6 tbls) olive oil**

For the stuffing:
○ **24 stoned black olives**
○ **60ml (4 tbls) breadcrumbs**
○ **60ml (4 tbls) parsley, coarsely chopped**
○ **3 peeled cloves garlic**
○ **45ml (3 tbls) pine kernels**
○ **30ml (2 tbls) capers**
○ **30ml (2 tbls) olive oil**
○ **15ml (1 tbls) anchovy paste**
○ **juice of ½ a lemon**
○ **pepper**

1. Clean the sardines, cut off the heads, wash under cold running water and dry on kitchen paper. Split them open down the belly without separating the fillets and remove the backbone. Reserve.
2. Prepare the stuffing: place the capers, pine kernels, olives and 30ml (2 tbls) of breadcrumbs in an electric mixer. Pour into a salad bowl and add the rest of the breadcrumbs, chopped parsley, anchovy paste, lemon juice and oil. Crush the garlic and mix the juice into the stuffing. Season with pepper and mix thoroughly to obtain a smooth paste.
3. Set the oven to 230°C (450°F; gas mark 8). Oil a baking dish with 30ml (2 tbls) of oil.
4. Stuff the sardines: place ½ tsp of stuffing in each fish cavity and press the sides together to prevent the stuffing from coming out while cooking. Arrange the sardines on the baking dish in a single layer.
5. Sprinkle with crumbled bay leaves and breadcrumbs. Pour over the rest of the oil and bake for 15 minutes until the breadcrumbs are brown.
6. Serve hor or warm.

Sardines Rôties au Jus de Citron

Serves 4. Preparation: 15 min Cooking: 15 min

Baked Sardines with Lemon Juice

★

○ **1.2kg (2½ lb) sardines**
○ **juice of 2 lemons**
○ **45ml (3 tbls) dry white wine**
○ **100ml (3½ fl oz) olive oil**
○ **3 bay leaves**
○ **1 sprig rosemary**
○ **salt and pepper**

1. Clean the sardines, cut off the heads and wash under cold running water. Dry on kitchen paper. Crumble the bay leaves and rosemary and mix well.
2. Set the oven to 230°C (450°F; gas mark 8). Oil an ovenproof dish with 30ml (2 tbls) oil, arrange the sardines in it, season with salt and pepper and sprinkle with the bay leaves and rosemary. Pour over the lemon juice, white wine and the rest of the oil. Bake for 15 minutes.
3. Serve very hot in the same dish.

The dogfish, though beautiful with its long thin speckled body, will always be found skinless and headless at the fishmongers. This is due to its remarkable resemblance to a small shark, which might put some customers off. Its boneless flesh is rather bland and requires a spicy sauce.

John Dory – its scientific name is Zenus faber (it was sacred to Zeus) – is a strange and unique fish owing its name to a legend: caught by St Peter, it started to complain; St Peter then released it, leaving on its sides his fingerprints. Ever since then it has always complained when taken out of the water!

John Dory is probably one of the finest of fish with its succulent and boneless flesh, comparable to sole and turbot for quality. Recipes for these are suitable for John Dory, and it is also marvellous in bouillabaisse.

Saint-Pierre aux Poireaux (p57)▶

Sardines au Laurier

Serves 4. Preparation: 25 min Cooking: 20 min

Sardines with Bay Leaves

★

○ 1.2kg (2½ lb) sardines
○ 30 bay leaves
○ 100g (4 oz) breadcrumbs
○ 150ml (5 fl oz) olive oil
○ salt and pepper

1. Clean the sardines, cut the heads off, rinse quickly and dry on kitchen paper. Split them open, press gently and remove the backbone, then close the fish again.
2. Oil an ovenproof dish with 30ml (2 tbls) of oil and arrange the fish in a single layer. Season. Scatter on the bay leaves and sprinkle with vinegar.
3. Set the oven to 220°C (425°F; gas mark 7). Mix the breadcrumbs and the rest of the oil together with a fork. If the paste is too thick, add a drop more oil. Coat the sardines with this paste and bake for 20 minutes until the fish is crisp and golden.
4. Serve at once.

Serve with a mixed salad, spring onions and lemon quarters.

Sardines Froides au Fenouil

Serves 6. Preparation and cooking: 1¼ hr

Chilled Sardines with Fennel

★★

○ 1.5kg (3¼ lb) sardines
○ 15ml (1 tbls) fennel seeds
○ 60ml (4 tbls) breadcrumbs
○ 45ml (3 tbls) olive oil
○ salt

For the sauce:
○ 2 tins peeled tomatoes, 750g (1½ lb) each
○ 4 onions
○ 100ml (3½ fl oz) vinegar
○ 100ml (3½ fl oz) white vermouth
○ 15ml (1 tbls) tomato purée
○ 45ml (3 tbls) olive oil
○ 1 pinch sugar
○ 1 small pimento
○ salt and pepper

1. Peel and finely chop the onions. Open the tins of tomatoes, reserve the juice and roughly chop the tomatoes.
2. To prepare the sauce: gently sauté the onions in 45ml (3 tbls) of oil for 5 minutes. When they are a nice golden colour, add the vinegar and reduce over a high heat. Add the vermouth, leave to evaporate, and then pour in the crushed tomatoes and their juice. Season, and add the tomato purée, sugar and the crushed pimento. Cook gently for 30 minutes, stirring from time to time with a wooden spoon.
3. Meanwhile, clean the sardines and cut off the heads. Rinse under cold water and dry. Oil a baking dish and set the oven to 230°C (450°F; gas mark 8).
4. When the sauce is cooked, pour into the dish and spread out with a spatula. Place the sardines on top in a single layer. Season with salt, sprinkle with fennel seeds, breadcrumbs and the rest of the oil. Bake for 25 minutes.
5. When ready, arrange the fish on a serving dish and leave to cool.

The sardines will be even better if you prepare them the day before serving.

The pike-perch, much prized by the Hungarians who call it fogash, *has left its birth-place – Lake Balaton – to inhabit the Rhine and Rhone valleys. It is as delicious as pike, but without the bones, and may be prepared in the same way as bass, pike, trout or salmon.*

Blood appearing at the gills of fish like sardines, herring, red mullet or anchovy is a sign of decomposition, whereas with other fish, such as the bass or dorado, it is a sign of freshness.

Sardines Marinées aux Oignons
Marinated Sardines with Onions

Serves 4. Preparation: 15 min
Cooking: 10 min Marinade: 24 hr
★

○ **1kg (2¼ lb) sardines**
○ **4 chopped onions**
○ **400ml (14 fl oz) wine vinegar**
○ **40g (2 oz) pine kernels**
○ **45ml (3 tbls) flour**
○ **200ml (7 fl oz) peanut oil**
○ **100ml (3½ fl oz) olive oil**
○ **5ml (1 tsp) fine salt**

1. Scale the sardines, cut off the heads, clean and wash under cold water. Dry on kitchen paper and dip in flour seasoned with salt.
2. Heat the peanut oil in a frying pan and sauté the fish for 1 minute on each side until golden and place on kitchen paper. Discard the oil.
3. Gently sauté the onions in fresh oil without browning and sprinkle with the vinegar, bring to the boil over a high heat and allow to boil for 1 minute.
4. Arrange the sardines in a deep dish and sprinkle with the pine kernels and onion-vinegar mixture. Cover and leave to marinate in the fridge for at least 24 hours before serving.

This is a delicious first course for spring or summer.

Saumon aux Raisins de Smyrne
Salmon with Sultanas

Serves 4. Preparation: 10 min
Cooking: 30 min
★

○ **4 slices of salmon, 200g (7 oz) each**
○ **1 400g (14 oz) tin peeled tomatoes**
○ **50g (2 oz) sultanas**
○ **75ml (5 tbls) oil**
○ **1 clove garlic**
○ **1 onion**
○ **15ml (1 tbls) parsley, coarsely chopped**
○ **15ml (1 tbls) basil, coarsely chopped**
○ **salt and pepper**

1. Wash the slices of salmon and dry on kitchen paper. Peel and finely chop the garlic and onion. Crush the peeled tomatoes to a fine purée.
2. Heat the oil in a saucepan and gently sauté the garlic and onion for a few minutes. Add the tomatoes. Bring to the boil and put in the slices of salmon. Season with salt and pepper. Cover and leave to cook gently for 25 minutes.
3. Meanwhile, soak the sultanas in warm water for 15 minutes. Drain and add to the saucepan.
4. 5 minutes before it is ready, sprinkle with the chopped parsley and basil. Arrange the fish on a serving dish, pour over the sauce and serve at once.

Can also be served chilled. This recipe is suitable for salted or fresh cod.

With freshly-caught fish the ideal court-bouillon *is sea water or salted water – 25g (1 oz) coarse salt for 1 litre (2 pints) of water: perch, cod or haddock do not need more.*

For salted cod, turbot, brill and sole, prepare a stock with 250ml (1½ pints) of milk for 2 litres (4 pints) of salted water and a few lemon slices.

A court-bouillon with vinegar is particularly suitable for hake, carp and mackerel. For 2 litres (4 pints) of water you need 100ml (3½ fl oz) of vinegar, 2 carrots, 2 onions, 6 sprigs of parsley, 1 sprig of thyme, 1 bay leaf, 2 cloves, 30ml (2 tbls) of coarse salt and 12 peppercorns.

For pike-perch, perch, trout, salmon and eel, replace the vinegar with white wine: 1 litre (2 pints) of water for 1 litre (2 pints) of wine. Eel, pike and carp can also be cooked in red wine in the proportions two-thirds water to one-third wine.

Saumon Cru au Poivre Vert

Serves 4. Preparation: 15 min, 15 min before serving

Raw Salmon with Green Pepper

★

○ **800g (2 lb) fresh salmon**
○ **24 green peppercorns**
○ **30ml (2 tbls) olive oil**
○ **1 green lemon**

1. Ask your fishmonger to give you a piece of salmon near the head, and to remove the skin and cut it into fillets, removing the backbone.
2. Check that no bones are left. Use a tweezer if necessary.
3. Slice the fillets of salmon finely (so thin they are transparent) and arrange on decorated plates. Brush with olive oil and place on a plate in the fridge for 15 minutes.
4. Crush the peppercorns in a mortar. Just before serving, sprinkle the fish with pepper and garnish with lemon quarters.

Serve with hot toast. No need for butter or salt. It is easier to cut the salmon into thin slices if you put it in the fridge beforehand: its flesh will then be firmer.

Saumon à l'Unilatérale

Serves 4. Preparation: 10 min Cooking: 30 sec

One-way Salmon

★

○ **800g (2 lb) fresh salmon**
○ **10ml (2 tsp) oil**

To serve:
○ **100g (4 oz) butter**
○ **1 lemon**
○ **salt and pepper**

1. Ask your fishmonger for a piece of salmon near the head. Ask him to remove the skin and cut it into two fillets, removing the backbone.
2. Light the grill. Check that no bones are left, using a pair of tweezers if necessary.
3. Cut each fillet in half and brush with oil.
4. Gently melt the butter in a saucepan. Cut the lemon into quarters.
5. Grill the fillets for 30 seconds on one side only. The salmon scallops should be golden on one side, opaque in the middle and transparent on top, hence its name 'one-way'.
6. Arrange the slices on individual plates and pour the melted butter into a sauceboat.
7. Serve at once, garnished with lemon, salt and pepper. Hand the butter separately.

This Scandinavian-style salmon is delicious simply served with melted butter, but you can add leaf spinach or steamed potatoes. This kind of cooking can also be done in a non-stick frying pan, without fat.

Nowadays many restaurants serve lightly cooked or even raw fish: salmon in thin scallops, diced bass, dorado in thin slices, salted small sardines. If you want to try it at home, make sure the fish is absolutely fresh, caught less than 48 hours before.

Sardines Marinées aux Oignons (p61) ➤

Filets de Sole aux Fines Herbes

Serves 4. Preparation and cooking: 20 min

Sole Fillets with Chives

★★

- ○ **8 sole fillets**
- ○ **150g (5 oz) butter**
- ○ **100g (4 oz) cream**
- ○ **30ml (2 tbls) chives, coarsely chopped**
- ○ **30ml (2 tbls) flour**
- ○ **salt**

1. Wash the sole fillets under cold running water and drain. Dip in 22ml (1½ tbls) of flour and shake to remove excess. Reserve.
2. Melt 100g (4 oz) butter in a frying pan large enough to contain all the fillets and sauté for 2 minutes on each side until golden. Season with salt. Lift out the fish and keep warm.
3. Mash the remaining butter with 7ml (½ tbls) of flour. Put in the frying pan, stirring well with a wooden spoon, and pour in the cream. Allow to cook for 5 minutes, stirring continuously.
4. Return the sole fillets to the frying pan, mix well with the sauce, and serve immediately.

Filets de Sole au Vermouth

Serves 4. Preparation: 10 min Cooking: 12 min

Sole Fillets with Vermouth

★★

- ○ **8 sole fillets**
- ○ **100ml (3½ fl oz) white vermouth**
- ○ **100ml (3½ fl oz) dry white wine**
- ○ **80g (3 oz) butter**
- ○ **juice of 1 green lemon**
- ○ **2 cloves**
- ○ **2 pinches cinnamon**
- ○ **salt and pepper**
- ○ **nutmeg**

1. Wash the fillets and dry on kitchen paper. Set the oven to 220°C (425°F; gas mark 7).
2. Butter an ovenproof dish with 20g (1 oz) butter and arrange the fillets in a single layer. Season with salt, pepper and nutmeg and sprinkle with cinnamon. Add the cloves and 20g (1 oz) butter cut into knobs. Pour over the vermouth and wine and cover the dish with aluminium foil.
3. Bake for 10 minutes then take the dish out of the oven. Drain the fish and place on a serving dish, keeping it warm.
4. Pour the cooking juice into a saucepan and reduce by half over a high heat for approximately 2 minutes, then add the lemon juice. Remove from the heat and beat in the last of the butter. Pour over the fish and serve immediately.

There are at least 6 varieties of sole, but the true sole is without doubt the best. Its head is round, its mouth has the shape of a parrot's beak and its colouring varies from pale grey to dark brown with blackish irregular markings, giving it the quality of the chameleon. Its two gills are on the blind – belly – side and their diameter is different, but the largest remains smaller than the eyes. This is an important detail which enables you to distinguish it from the sole pôle, *whose largest gill is bigger than its eyes. Another detail to note: the true sole has a black mark near its right front fin whereas for the* sole pôle, *it is placed in the middle.*

Other types of sole are the lemon sole, of yellowish appearance, the torbay sole or 'witch sole', a beautiful pinkish-purple fish, and the megrim, whiff, sail-fluke or west-coast sole.

Always choose thick fleshy soles. When it carries eggs in January or February, its flesh is soft. The best sole comes from the Channel, and is called the Dover sole.

You can prepare a delicious fry-up with sole fillets: cut the fillets slantwise into thin strips, season and dip in flour; shake and fry for one minute. Drain and serve hot with lemon.

Soles Meunière

Serves 2. Preparation: 5 min Cooking: 6 min

Sole Meunière

★

- ○ **2 soles**
- ○ **30ml (2 tbls) flour**
- ○ **100ml (3½ fl oz) peanut oil**
- ○ **80g (3 oz) butter, lightly salted**
- ○ **juice of 1 lemon**
- ○ **15ml (1 tbls) parsley, coarsely chopped**
- ○ **salt and white pepper**

1. Ask your fishmonger to skin and clean the sole.
2. Wash the fish under running water and dry on kitchen paper. Dip in flour and shake to remove excess.
3. Heat the oil in a non-stick frying pan and gently fry the fish for 3 minutes on each side, turning once. Season with salt.
4. Meanwhile, cut the butter into small knobs and put in a saucepan with the lemon juice. Place over a very low heat, on an asbestos sheet if possible. As soon as the butter is soft, not completely melted, remove from the heat and whisk until frothy. Season with pepper.
5. When the sole are golden-brown, place on kitchen paper to drain and arrange on a serving dish; sprinkle with parsley, pour the seasoned butter over the sole and serve immediately.

Sole Meunière prepared in this way is light and crisp as it has not cooked in butter. This recipe is suitable for red mullet, salmon steak, cod or hake, and the fillet of dab or brill. Garnish with slices of lemon and small steamed potatoes. If you have several sole to prepare, keep them in a warm oven.

Soles au Varech

Serves 6. Preparation and cooking: 25 min

Sole in Seaweed

★★★

- ○ **3 soles, 500g (1 lb) each**
- ○ **1 handful of seaweed**
- ○ **4 shallots**
- ○ **200ml (7 fl oz) dry white wine**
- ○ **1 bunch of chives**
- ○ **100g (4 oz) butter**
- ○ **100g (4 oz) cream**
- ○ **salt and pepper**

1. Ask your fishmonger to skin the sole and cut into fillets.
2. Use a double saucepan or a couscous dish. Bring water to boil in the bottom part; arrange the seaweed in the top part, and place on top the sole fillets folded in two, shiny side inwards. Do not put above the water yet.
3. Prepare the sauce: peel and finely chop the shallots. Put in a saucepan with the white wine and boil for 5 minutes approximately until there is only about 15ml (1 tbls) of liquid left.
4. When the water is boiling, put the top part of the saucepan in place and allow to cook for 5 minutes.
5. Meanwhile, add the butter to the sauce and stir in the cream, whisking continuously over a low heat. When ready, season with salt and pepper. Remove from the heat. Chop the chives and add to the sauce. Pour into a sauce-boat.
6. Lift out the sole fillets, arrange on their seaweed bed on a serving dish and serve with the sauce separately.

This recipe is suitable for dab or John Dory fillets. Ask your fishmonger for the seaweed.

Filets de Sole Poêlés au Citron

Serves 4. Preparation: 5 min Cooking: 10 min

Fillets of Sole Fried with Lemon

○ **4 soles, 300g (11 oz) each**
○ **120g (4 oz) butter**
○ **45ml (3 tbls) flour**
○ **45ml (3 tbls) parsley, coarsely chopped**
○ **juice of 1 lemon**
○ **salt and pepper**

1. Skin the sole, clean and cut off the heads. Cut into fillets. All this can be done by your fishmonger. Rinse quickly under cold water, dry and season with salt and pepper. Roll in flour and shake to remove excess.
2. Heat 80g (3 oz) of butter in a frying pan and gently fry the fillets for 4 minutes on each side: the butter must not burn and should keep its golden colour. Lift out the fish and arrange on a serving dish. Keep the dish warm.
3. Add the lemon juice to the butter used for frying, remove from the heat and put in the last of the butter. Stir with a wooden spoon and pour this butter over the fillets. Sprinkle with parsley and serve at once.

Soles Colbert

Serves 4. Preparation and cooking: 35 min

Sole Colbert

★★

○ **4 soles, 300g (11 oz) each**
○ **45ml (3 tbls) flour**
○ **45ml (3 tbls) breadcrumbs**
○ **2 eggs**
○ **30ml (2 tbls) oil**
○ **30ml (2 tbls) water**
○ **125g (4 oz) soft butter**
○ **30ml (2 tbls) parsley, coarsely chopped**
○ **30ml (2 tbls) lemon juice**
○ **oil for frying**
○ **salt and pepper**

1. Skin the sole, clean through the gills, rinse under cold water and dry on kitchen paper. Make a cut down the centre of each sole, along the backbone. Slide the knife in so that the flesh is eased away from the bone, without removing the fillet. Snip the backbone at each end, this makes it easily removable when the fish is cooked. Roll back the cut edges to make an opening in the fish.
2. Place the flour in a soup dish, breadcrumbs in another and in a third the eggs beaten with water and oil. Season with salt and pepper.
3. Season the soles with salt and pepper both inside and out. Dip them in the flour, then in the egg and finally in the breadcrumbs.
4. Heat the oil for frying and gently fry the sole for 4 minutes on each side over a low heat. Lift out and remove the backbone with a small knife.
5. Arrange the fish on a serving dish and keep warm while you prepare the butter *maître d'hôtel*: mash the soft butter with the parsley and lemon juice. Season with salt and pepper. Stuff each sole with the butter *maître d'hôtel* and serve immediately.

Serve with lemon quarters and small boiled or steamed potatoes.

The fresher a sole is, the more difficult it is to skin. Generally the fishmonger does it, but if you want to do it yourself, lay the fish on a board dark side up; cut off the tail, loosen the black skin at the cut where the fish was cleaned, grasp the tail end of the skin with the corner of a tea towel and pull it off.

If the sole is prepared in fillets, the white skin should be removed in the same way. To cut into fillets, trim the fins with scissors. Run the point of the knife down the backbone between the fillets and the backbone, until the fillet is detached.

Filets de Sole à la Crème

Serves 4. Preparation: 10 min Cooking: 40 min

Sole Fillets with Cream

★★★

○ **4 soles, 300g (11 oz) each**
○ **150g (5 oz) cream**
○ **1 sliced lemon**
○ **60g (2 oz) butter**
○ **salt and pepper**

For the stock:
○ **2 carrots**
○ **1 onion**
○ **200ml (7 fl oz) dry white wine**
○ **1 bouquet garni: 6 sprigs parsley, 1 bay leaf, 1 sprig thyme**
○ **salt and peppercorns**

1. Skin the soles and cut into fillets. Keep the heads and bones. Rinse the fillets under running water and dry. Peel and finely chop the onion and carrots.
2. Prepare the stock: put the heads and bones in a saucepan with the onion, carrots and bouquet garni. Pour in the wine and 400ml (1 pint) of water, and season with salt and pepper. Bring to the boil and leave to cook gently for 20 minutes.
3. Set the oven to 220°C (425°F; gas mark 7). Season the fillets with salt and pepper. Butter a baking dish with 20g (1 oz) of butter and lay in the fish. Strain the stock over and cover with aluminium foil. Bake for 12 minutes.
4. When the fillets are cooked, lift them out, arrange on a serving dish and keep warm. Pour the cooking liquid into a saucepan and reduce over a high heat until you have about 100ml (3½ fl oz) of liquid left. Add the cream, reduce for 3 minutes, stirring continuously, then remove from the heat and add the rest of the butter in knobs. Season with salt and pepper.
5. Pour the cream sauce over the fillets and serve at once with lemon slices.

Soles aux Amandes et aux Herbes

Serves 4. Preparation: 10 min Cooking: 25 min Marinade: 15 min

Sole with Almonds and Herbs

★★

○ **4 soles, 300g (11 oz) each**
○ **60ml (4 tbls) flaked almonds**
○ **120g (4 oz) butter**
○ **2 eggs**
○ **10 sprigs parsley**
○ **2 sprigs tarragon**
○ **2 sprigs dill**
○ **125g (4 oz) cream**
○ **juice of 1 lemon**
○ **salt and pepper**

1. Skin the sole, clean and cut off the tails and fins. Rinse the fish under running water and dry. Place in a dish and sprinkle with lemon juice. Cover and leave to marinate for 15 minutes.
2. Crumble 45ml (3 tbls) of almonds with your fingers and put on a plate. When the sole has marinated for 15 minutes, drain and roll the fish in the almonds, pressing slightly to make them stick.
3. Melt 80g (3 oz) of butter in a frying pan and gently fry the sole for 3 minutes on each side until golden. Drain and keep the fish warm. Set the oven to 200°C (400°F; gas mark 6), butter a baking dish with 20g (1 oz) of butter and arrange the sole in it.
4. Finely chop the parsley, tarragon and dill. Beat the eggs, add the cream and herbs and season. Pour the mixture over the sole. Sprinkle with the remainder of the almonds and add a few knobs of butter. Bake for 15 minutes and serve at once in the cooking dish.

Preparing a stock could not be simpler: place in a saucepan 1 onion, 1 carrot, the white of a leek and a stick of celery, finely chopped. Add 3 sprigs of parsley, a clove, ½ bay leaf, a sprig of fennel and a sprig of thyme. Put the heads and bones if the fish is filleted, if whole, the head and bones of 1 or 2 soles will be sufficient. Cover with water and simmer for 20 minutes. Strain and add salt, pepper and the juice of ½ lemon. If you need a smaller quantity of liquid, reduce as required.

Filets de Sole aux Nouilles Fraîches

Serves 4. Preparation and cooking: 30 min

Sole Fillets with Fresh Tagliatelle

- ○ **8 fillets of sole**
- ○ **8 scallops**
- ○ **250g (8 oz) cream**
- ○ **30ml (2 tbls) white vermouth**
- ○ **5ml (1 tsp) tomato purée**
- ○ **250g (8 oz) tagliatelle**
- ○ **30g (1 oz) butter**
- ○ **nutmeg**
- ○ **salt and pepper**

1. Ask your fishmonger to prepare the scallops. Wash the fillets under running water and dry on kitchen paper. Season with salt, pepper and nutmeg. Place a fillet around each scallop, shiny side inside and secure with a toothpick or cocktail stick.
2. Put the cream and vermouth into a saucepan large enough to contain the fish, lay in the fillets, season with salt and pepper, bring to the boil and cook gently for 5 minutes. Remove the fillets, drain and keep warm.
3. Return the saucepan to a low heat and add the tomato purée. Boil down to half the liquid for about 10 minutes.
4. Meanwhile, boil some water in a large saucepan, add salt and plunge in the tagliatelle. Cook for 5 to 6 minutes, until it is *al dente*. Drain, stir in the butter and arrange on a serving dish. Place the fillets on top, coat with the sauce and serve immediately.

Serve with freshly ground pepper. Fresh tagliatelle can sometimes be bought in delicatessen shops.

Sole au Muscadet

Serves 2. Preparation and cooking: 35 min

Sole with Muscadet

★ ★

- ○ **1 large sole, about 600g (1½ lb)**
- ○ **250ml (9 fl oz) Muscadet**
- ○ **60g (2 oz) butter**
- ○ **2 shallots**
- ○ **30ml (2 tbls) cream**
- ○ **salt and pepper**

1. Skin, clean and dry the sole. Peel and finely chop the shallots. Set the oven to 200°C (400°F; gas mark 6).
2. Butter an ovenproof dish large enough to contain the fish. Sprinkle with the chopped shallots, then place the fish in and season with salt and pepper. Pour over the white wine, add a few knobs of butter, cover with aluminium foil and bake for 15 minutes.
3. When the fish is cooked, arrange on a serving dish, cover with aluminium foil and keep warm in the oven, with the heat turned off and the door ajar.
4. Place the cooking dish over a high heat and reduce the liquid until you have 60ml (4 tbls) left. Whisk in the cream and leave to cook gently for 2 minutes. Remove from the heat and stir in the remaining butter, beating constantly.
5. Strain this sauce over the sole and serve at once.

When in season sprinkle with fresh chopped tarragon or chives.

You can add wine, champagne, vermouth or cream to the stock which can be used to cook whole fish or fillets (baked or stewed). Once cooked, reduce the liquid, add the butter, egg yolks or cream to thicken it and season with chives or herbs of your choice.

Thon à l'Aigre-Douce

Serves 4. Preparation: 10 min Cooking: 25 min

Sweet and Sour Tuna

★★

- ○ **4 slices of tuna, 200g (7 oz) each**
- ○ **4 ripe tomatoes**
- ○ **100ml (3½ fl oz) vinegar**
- ○ **15ml (1 tbls) parsley, coarsely chopped**
- ○ **15ml (1 tbls) basil, coarsely chopped**
- ○ **1 clove garlic**
- ○ **15ml (1 tbls) capers**
- ○ **15ml (1 tbls) flour**
- ○ **45ml (3 tbls) olive oil**
- ○ **1 small pimento**
- ○ **2.5ml (½ tsp) sugar**
- ○ **oil for frying**
- ○ **salt**

1. Wash and dry the fish on kitchen paper. Dip in flour and reserve.
2. Scald the tomatoes for 10 seconds in boiling water, drain, refresh in cold water, peel and remove the seeds. Crush to a pulp. Peel and finely chop the garlic.
3. Heat the oil in a large frying pan and fry the fish for 1 minute on each side until golden. Lift out, drain on kitchen paper and keep warm. Discard the oil and wipe the pan.
4. Heat the olive oil and gently fry the garlic, crushed pimento, basil, parsley and capers. Add the vinegar and reduce over a high heat, then add the tomatoes and sugar. Mix well with a wooden spoon and season with salt. Lay in the slices of fish, cover and allow to simmer for 10 minutes, turning the fish after 5 minutes.
5. Serve hot or chilled.

Thon Grillé aux Herbes

Serves 4. Preparation: 10 min
Marinade: 1 hr Cooking: 10 min

Grilled Tuna with Herbs

★

- ○ **4 slices of tuna, 200g (7 oz) each**
- ○ **juice of 1 lemon**
- ○ **2 bay leaves**
- ○ **4 sage leaves**
- ○ **4 basil leaves**
- ○ **10 sprigs parsley**
- ○ **2.5ml (½ tsp) rosemary**
- ○ **2.5ml (½ tsp) thyme**
- ○ **3 anchovy fillets in oil**
- ○ **1 clove garlic (peeled)**
- ○ **30ml (2 tbls) oil**
- ○ **salt and pepper**

1. Wash the fish under cold running water and dry. Finely chop the sage, basil, parsley, thyme, rosemary and bay leaves. Crush the garlic and finely chop the anchovy fillets.
2. Place the fish in a large dish, season with salt and pepper and sprinkle with lemon juice.
3. Mix together the herbs, garlic and anchovies with 30ml (2 tbls) oil. Coat the fish with this mixture on both sides and allow to marinate for 1 hour.
4. When ready to cook, lift out the fish (do not remove the herbs) and grill for 5 minutes on each side. Serve with a salad.

This recipe is also suitable for cod and bonito.

Tuna must be absolutely fresh: this is the only fish which can cause serious food-poisoning when it is not fresh. The best is red tuna whose bright red, firm, smooth, shiny flesh is a sign of freshness. White tuna is rather tasteless and is used mostly for pickling.

The turbot with its firm white flesh is much sought after, but unfortunately it is very expensive as there is about 50% waste. It has a lozenge-shaped body and a knobbly, scale-free skin. With strong teeth and prominent eyes, it can reach up to 2m in length and 40kg (80 lb) in weight.

Small turbot (turbotin) can be prepared in fillets, like the sole, brill and dab. When bigger, it is sliced and grilled or poached and served with beurre blanc *or hollandaise sauce.*

Sole au Muscadet (p69) ▶

Thon à la Livournaise

Tuna Italian-Style

Serves 4. Preparation: 15 min Cooking: 15 min

★

- ○ **4 slices of tuna, 200g (7 oz) each**
- ○ **1 400g (14 oz) tin peeled tomatoes**
- ○ **150ml (5 fl oz) oil**
- ○ **100g (4 oz) black olives**
- ○ **50g (2 oz) capers**
- ○ **2 cloves garlic**
- ○ **salt and pepper**

1. Rinse the fish under cold running water and dry on kitchen paper.
2. Crush the tomatoes to a fine purée. Stone and roughly chop the olives. Peel and finely chop the garlic.
3. Pour the oil into a large frying pan, add the tomatoes, capers, olives, garlic and the fish. Season. Place the frying pan on a strong flame and cook the tuna for 5 to 6 minutes on each side, depending on its thickness. Serve hot with a mixed salad.

Red mullet can be prepared in the same way.

Truites au Beurre Rouge

Trout with Butter and Wine

Serves 4. Preparation: 10 min Marinade: 2 hr
Cooking: 20 min

★ ★

- ○ **4 good-sized trout**
- ○ **½ litre (18 fl oz) red wine**
- ○ **2 shallots**
- ○ **1 sprig thyme**
- ○ **4 sprigs parsley**
- ○ **125g (4 oz) butter**
- ○ **1 pinch sugar**
- ○ **salt and pepper**

1. Clean and rinse the fish under cold running water and dry. Season with salt.
2. Butter a flameproof dish large enough to contain the fish without overlapping. Peel and finely chop the shallots, scatter in the bottom of the dish and place the trout on top. Sprinkle with thyme and parsley and cover with the red wine. Leave to marinate in the fridge for 2 hours.
3. After 2 hours, place the dish over a low heat. At the first sign of boiling, reduce the heat, season with salt and cover the dish with aluminium foil. Allow to simmer for 12 minutes then remove from the heat.
4. Arrange the trout on a serving dish, cover with foil and keep warm over a saucepan full of hot water.
5. Return the cooking dish to a high heat, add the sugar, remove the thyme and parsley and boil down until you have roughly 30ml (2 tbls) of liquid left. Remove from the heat. Cut the butter into small knobs, add to the dish and allow the butter to melt slowly while mixing with a wooden spoon. Season with pepper and pour over the trout. Serve at once.

Thin slices of apple fried in butter or potatoes boiled in their jackets go very well with this recipe. Choose a full-bodied wine to cook this dish and serve it with the same.

Small bass or two soles can be prepared in the same way without marinating.

Truites aux Amandes

Serves 4. Preparation: 10 min Cooking: 15 min

Trout with Almonds

★★

○ **4 trout, 250g (8 oz) each**
○ **120g (4 oz) almonds, shredded**
○ **200ml (7 fl oz) milk**
○ **15ml (1 tbls) flour**
○ **15ml (1 tbls) oil**
○ **150g (5 oz) butter**
○ **salt and pepper**

1. Clean the trout and rinse under cold running water. Dry on kitchen paper. Dip the fish first in the milk and then in flour and shake to remove excess.
2. Heat the oil in a frying pan and add 100g (4 oz) of butter. When melted, fry the fish for 5 minutes on each side, on a low heat to prevent the butter from turning black. Lift out, arrange on a serving dish, season and keep warm. Discard the butter and wipe the frying pan.
3. Melt the remaining butter and gently fry the almonds for approximately 2 minutes, until golden, then pour over the trout together with the butter and serve at once.

Serve with lemon quarters.

Truites à la Moutarde et à la Crème

Serves 4. Preparation: 10 min Cooking: 25 min

Trout with Mustard and Cream

★

○ **4 trout, 250g (8 oz) each**
○ **12 thin slices bacon**
○ **200g (7 oz) cream**
○ **10ml (2 tsp) mustard**
○ **juice of 1 lemon**
○ **salt and white pepper**

1. Clean and rinse the trout under cold running water and dry on kitchen paper. Season with salt and pepper inside and out. Sprinkle with lemon juice and coat with the mustard.
2. Set the oven to 220°C (425°F; gas mark 7). Place the 6 slices of bacon on the bottom of an ovenproof dish and arrange the trout on top. Lay on the remaining bacon. Cover with aluminium foil and bake for 20 minutes.
3. When the fish is cooked, remove the foil and add the cream. Leave to cook for a further 5 minutes.
4. Lift out the fish and place on a serving dish. Pour over the juice and serve immediately.

Small steamed potatoes go very well with this dish.

Only the freshly caught trout can be prepared au bleu. *This rather barbarous but simple preparation, which is considered the best, requires live trout, prepared a few minutes before serving.*

Stun the fish by banging their heads against the table, then clean them quickly through the gills. Whatever you do, do not scrub, rinse or wipe them: it is this slimy coating which gives the blue colour. Drop them in boiling salted water and simmer for 7 minutes, for a 180g (6 oz) trout. Lift out and arrange on a dish covered with a tea towel: the trout will have turned a lovely blue colour.

Serve with melted butter and lemon quarters, or chilled with mayonnaise. This preparation au bleu *is suitable for other fish: pike, carp, fera and char when it is not too large.*

The vieille *trout is a lovely multicoloured fish which lives among seaweed off the Atlantic coast and feeds on shellfish. It can be grilled, or if small is excellent prepared in fish soup.*

Turbot aux Petits Oignons

Serves 4. Preparation: 15 min Cooking: 45 min

Turbot with Small Onions

★★

- ○ 1 1.5kg (3 lb) turbot
- ○ 20 small onions (or pickling onions)
- ○ 200ml (7 fl oz) dry white wine
- ○ 1 carrot
- ○ 3 tomatoes
- ○ 60ml (4 tbls) olive oil
- ○ juice of 1 lemon
- ○ 1 bouquet garni: bay leaf, 1 sprig thyme, 1 sprig rosemary
- ○ salt and peppercorns

1. Scrape the turbot, clean and rinse under running water and dry.
2. Peel and finely chop the onions. Clean and slice the carrot. Scald the tomatoes for 10 seconds. Peel, cut into halves and press to remove the seeds. Crush to a pulp.
3. Heat the oil in a frying pan and fry the onions until golden. Pour over the white wine and lemon juice, add the tomatoes, carrot, 6 peppercorns and bouquet garni. Season with salt and cover. Allow to simmer for 20 minutes.
4. When ready transfer the mixture from the frying pan to a saucepan (do not rinse the frying pan). Place the fish in the frying pan and pour over the sauce. Add a little water if necesssary to cover the fish. Cover and leave to cook gently for 20 minutes.
5. After 20 minutes remove the bouquet garni. Lift out the fish and arrange on a serving dish. Keep warm. Pass the sauce through a blender and pour over the turbot. Serve hot, warm or chilled.

Turbotin aux Trois Légumes

Serves 4. Preparation: 20 min Cooking: 40 min

Chicken Turbot with Vegetables

★★

- ○ 1 1.5kg (3 lb) chicken turbot
- ○ 2 carrots
- ○ 2 leeks
- ○ 2 celery sticks
- ○ 200ml (7 fl oz) dry white wine
- ○ 150g (5 oz) cream
- ○ 12 sprigs chervil
- ○ 50g (2 oz) butter
- ○ salt and pepper

1. Scrape, clean and rinse the turbot under running water. Dry on kitchen paper.
2. Set the oven to 220°C (425°F; gas mark 7). Peel, rinse and grate the carrots. Remove the outer green leaves of the leeks, wash and cut the white part into thin slices. Wash the sticks of celery and slice.
3. Butter a baking dish and cover the base with the chopped vegetables. Lay in the turbot and pour over the white wine. Season with salt and dot with butter. Cover the dish with aluminium foil and bake for 35 minutes.
4. When ready, lift out the turbot and arrange on a serving dish, removing its black skin. Garnish the fish with the vegetables, cover with foil and keep warm in the oven, switched off with the door ajar.
5. Put the baking dish on a medium heat, add the cream to the cooking liquid and boil for approximately 3 minutes until the sauce has reduced to a third.
6. Chop the chervil. When the sauce is ready, remove from the heat, add the chervil and season with pepper. Pour some of the sauce around the fish and the rest into a sauceboat. Serve immediately.

This recipe is also suitable for dab, brill or plaice.

With a flat fish like the sole and turbot, a white belly without markings is a sign of freshness.

Mixed Grill de Poissons Marinés (p76) ▶

Mixed Grill de Poissons Marinés

Mixed Grill of Marinated Fish

Serves 4. Preparation: 10 min
Marinade: 2 hr Cooking: 8 min
★

○ **4 thin slices tuna or swordfish**
○ **4 slices salmon**
○ **8 large Dublin Bay prawns**
○ **1 clove garlic (peeled)**
○ **juice of 1 lemon**
○ **200ml (7 fl oz) oil**
○ **salt and pepper**

1. Rinse the salmon, tuna or swordfish and Dublin Bay prawns. Dry on kitchen paper and place in a large dish.
2. Prepare the marinade: crush the garlic and keep the juice in a bowl. Add the oil and lemon juice and season. Beat with a fork and sprinkle over the fish. Leave to marinate for 2 hours in the fridge.
3. When ready, turn on the grill or prepare a barbecue. When the grill is hot, grill the fish and shellfish for 4 minutes on each side, sprinkling with the marinade.

Serve very hot with lemon quarters, small fresh onions or green salad.

Marmite Dieppoise

Dieppe Fish-Pot

Serves 6. Preparation and cooking: 1 hr
★★★

○ **2 soles, 250g (8 oz) each**
○ **2 turbot fillets, 500g (18 oz) each**
○ **3 small red mullet**
○ **1½ litres (3 pints) mussels**
○ **2 onions**
○ **2 shallots**
○ **2 leeks**
○ **1 celery stick**
○ **1 sprig thyme**
○ **150g (5 oz) cream**
○ **2 egg yolks**
○ **80g (3 oz) butter**
○ **15ml (1 tbls) chervil, coarsely chopped**
○ **salt and pepper**

1. Ask your fishmonger to clean the soles and cut them into fillets. Keep the heads and bones and if possible the turbot trimmings. Cut the fillets into thin slices. Cut off the heads of the red mullet and reserve.
2. Place the fish heads and trimmings in 2 litres (3½ pints) of cold water. Season with salt and bring to the boil. Leave to boil for 10 minutes then strain the stock and reserve.
3. Scrub and rinse the mussels. Cook over a high heat in a saucepan until the shells open and remove from the heat. Discard the empty shell of each mussel, strain the mussel liquor and reserve.
4. Peel and finely chop the onions, shallots, the white of the leeks and the celery.
5. Melt half of the butter in a saucepan and gently sauté the chopped vegetables without browning for about 5 minutes, then add the thyme and stock. Leave to boil for 10 minutes and strain. Add the mussel liquor and fish to the stock. Allow to simmer for 6 minutes, then lift out the fish and arrange in a deep dish or soup bowl. Add the mussels.
6. Whisk the cream and egg yolks together in a bowl. Remove the saucepan from the heat and stir in the mixture and the last of the butter. Coat the fish with this smooth sauce, sprinkle with chervil, season with pepper and serve at once.

Serve with small croûtons fried in butter.

There are two sorts of weever, the large and small one. With a big mouth and small head, it has stiff spines along the dorsal fin which are poisonous. Weever flesh is highly esteemed and is indispensable in a true bouillabaisse. It is as succulent as the sole and all recipes for sole are suitable.

Bouillabaisse
Bouillabaisse

Serves 6 to 8. Preparation: 25 min Cooking: 30 min

★★

- ○ **2.5kg (5½ lb) fresh fish: scorpion-fish, John Dory, weever, gurnard, conger eel, angler, sea-bass etc**
- ○ **12 small shellfish: crabs, prawns**
- ○ **1 chopped onion**
- ○ **1 leek, white part, chopped**
- ○ **4 cloves garlic, peeled**
- ○ **3 tomatoes**
- ○ **1 sprig fennel**
- ○ **1 sprig thyme**
- ○ **1 bay leaf**
- ○ **1 piece dried orange peel**
- ○ **200ml (7 fl oz) olive oil**
- ○ **4 pinches saffron**
- ○ **2.5 litres (4 pints) boiling water**
- ○ **salt and pepper**

To garnish
- ○ **24 slices of toast**

1. Scale and clean the fish. Rinse under running water and chop the large ones into pieces. Peel the tomatoes, remove the seeds, and crush with a fork.
2. Heat the oil in a large saucepan and put in the onion, leek, tomatoes, crushed garlic, fennel, thyme, bay leaf and orange peel. Gently sauté for 8 minutes, mixing well, and add the crabs and prawns. Pour on the boiling water, season and boil for 5 minutes: this is to allow the oil and water to form an emulsion, giving a smooth sauce.
3. After 5 minutes, add the scorpion-fish, conger eel and angler. Allow to boil for 5 minutes then add the soft-fleshed fish: John Dory, weever, gurnard, sea-bass. Continue to boil for 10 minutes and taste for seasoning. Add the saffron and remove from the heat.
4. Serve the fish and soup in the same dish.

Bouillabaisse can be served with a sauce prepared as follows: crush together 2 small pimentos, 2 garlic cloves, salt, pepper, saffron and 50g (2 oz) white bread soaked in milk – or even better – soaked in the bouillabaisse stock. Blend finely then beat in 250ml (9 fl oz) olive oil, as for mayonnaise.

Waterzoï
Flemish Fish-Pot

Serves 6. Preparation and cooking: 1 hr

★★★

- ○ **2kg (4½ lb) white fish: whiting, conger, dorado, gurnard, angler, John Dory, brill**
- ○ **1 celery stick**
- ○ **3 carrots**
- ○ **3 leeks**
- ○ **2 onions chopped into 4**
- ○ **juice of ½ lemon**
- ○ **250ml (9 fl oz) dry white wine**
- ○ **1 sprig thyme**
- ○ **1 bay leaf**
- ○ **6 sprigs parsley**
- ○ **2 egg yolks**
- ○ **125g (4 oz) cream**
- ○ **30ml (2 tbls) chopped chives**
- ○ **salt and pepper**

1. Skin or scale the fish, clean and rinse under running water. Cut into thin slices. Put the heads and bones in a large saucepan and cover with 1 litre (2 pints) of water and the white wine. Add the thyme, bay leaf, parsley and onions, and season. Bring to the boil, then simmer for 20 minutes.
2. Meanwhile, boil 1 litre (2 pints) of water. Peel the carrots, leeks, and celery. Rinse quickly, shred the carrot, quarter the celery heart and roughly chop the leeks. When the water is boiling, add salt and the vegetables. Cook over a high heat with the lid on for 15 minutes.
3. When the fish stock is ready, strain and add to the vegetables. Bring back to the boil and add the fish. Leave to cook gently for 5 minutes, remove from the heat, lift out the fish and vegetables and arrange on a serving dish or in a soup-tureen.
4. Whisk together the cream, lemon juice and egg yolks, add to the stock, sprinkle with chives and pour over the fish and vegetables. Serve immediately.

Slices of toasted bread go very well with this Flemish dish. Suitable for river fish: eel, perch, pike etc.

Soupe de Poissons à la Tomate

Serves 4. Preparation: 25 min Cooking: 30 min

Fish Soup with Tomatoes

★★

- ○ 1.5kg (3¼ lb) fish: scorpion-fish, John Dory, weever, gurnard, conger, angler, whiting
- ○ 20 mussels
- ○ 4 Dublin Bay prawns
- ○ 1 very small octopus
- ○ 500g (1 lb) ripe tomatoes
- ○ 1 onion
- ○ 1 white of leek
- ○ 1 clove garlic
- ○ 1 small fresh red pimento
- ○ 150ml (5 fl oz) olive oil
- ○ 200ml (7 fl oz) dry white wine
- ○ salt and pepper

1. Scale the fish, clean, and cut the large ones into chunks of equal size. Rinse under running water and dry on kitchen paper. Scrub and rinse the mussels. Split the Dublin Bay prawns lengthwise. Clean the octopus, removing ink sac, rinse and chop into small pieces.
2. Wash the leek, peel and finely chop the leek, onion and garlic. Wash the tomatoes and crush to a pulp.
3. Heat the oil in a pan and gently sauté the garlic, onion, leek and small pimento. Add the octopus, mussels, Dublin Bay prawns and the fish with firm flesh, fry for another 5 minutes, then add the rest of the fish and cook for a further 5 minutes. Season with a little salt and pepper. Pour on the crushed tomatoes and white wine and cover with water. Leave to cook for 15 minutes over a high heat. Serve the soup in a bowl.

Serve this soup hot with toasted bread rubbed with garlic and, if you wish, an *aïoli* sauce or *rouille* sauce.

Bourride Provençale

Serves 6. Preparation and cooking: 1 hr 10 min

Provençal Fish-Pot

★★★

- ○ 2kg (3½ lb) white fish: whiting, bass, brill, turbot, conger, John Dory etc
- ○ 2 chopped onions
- ○ 2 leeks, white part only
- ○ 1 carrot
- ○ 1 celery stick
- ○ 1 sprig fennel
- ○ 2 cloves garlic
- ○ 1 bay leaf
- ○ 6 coriander seeds
- ○ 1 small piece of dried orange peel
- ○ 30ml (2 tbls) olive oil
- ○ salt

For the aïoli
- ○ 6 egg yolks
- ○ 400ml (14 fl oz) olive oil
- ○ 6 cloves garlic
- ○ salt

To garnish
- ○ 6 slices of bread toasted in the oven

1. Clean and scale the fish. Rinse under running water and cut into 4cm (2 inch) slices. Reserve the heads. Wash the leeks and carrot and chop finely together with the celery.
2. Place 30ml (2 tbls) of olive oil in a large saucepan, add the vegetables and fish heads and sauté gently for 5 minutes without browning. Add 2 litres (4 pints) of water and the whole garlic cloves, bay leaf, coriander seeds, fennel and orange peel. Season with salt, bring to the boil and allow to simmer for 20 minutes.
3. Meanwhile, prepare the *aïoli*: peel and crush the garlic with 4 pinches of salt, add the 2 egg yolks and the oil a drop at a time and beat the sauce like a mayonnaise. When the sauce is ready, take half of it and add the 4 remaining egg yolks, beating vigorously.
4. When the stock has cooked for 20 minutes, strain and return to the large saucepan, bring to the boil and add the fish in the following order: brill, turbot, conger, whiting, bass, John Dory. Allow to boil for 10 minutes.
5. Arrange the fish on a serving dish. Strain the stock and put the saucepan on a low heat. Add a ladle of stock to the *aïoli* sauce which has the 4 egg yolks, mix well and beat this mixture into the stock to obtain a smooth sauce; do not allow to boil. Pour into a soup-tureen and serve. Each guest will moisten his toasted bread with this stock and help himself to the fish with the *aïoli*.

The water can be replaced with the same quantity of dry white wine.

Wines: the Finishing Touch

Nowadays excellent quality table wines are within the reach of everyone, though you should expect to pay more for a good vintage wine from one of the famous vineyards, such as Nuits-St-Georges or Schloss Johannisberg Riesling. When buying French wine, look for the *Appellation Côntrolée* label, which is a guarantee of quality.

Below is a guide to the wines that go best with certain foods, but there are no absolute *rules* about which wine to serve with what food – in the end it is your palate that must decide. For a large, formal meal, certain wines traditionally follow each other through the menu and you could serve three or even four wines at one meal. In this case, it is usual to serve dry sherry with the soup, dry white wine with the fish course, claret or burgundy with the meat or game and a white dessert wine or medium sweet champagne with the dessert. For cheese, your guests would return to the claret or burgundy. Certain foods kill the flavour of wine and should therefore be avoided if you are planning to serve wine with the meal. Mint sauce, for example, or any salad with a strong vinaigrette dressing, will destroy the taste of the wine.

Remember that red wines are generally served *chambré*, or at room temperature, to bring out the flavour. Draw the cork at least three or four hours before you plan to drink the wine and let the bottle stand in the kitchen or a warm room. (Never be tempted into putting the bottle in hot water or in front of the fire – the flavour will be ruined.) The exception to the *chambré* rule is Beaujolais, which can be served cool – some people even serve it chilled. White or rosé wines are usually served chilled – the easiest way is to put them in the fridge an hour before serving, or plunge them into an ice bucket, if you have one. Champagne should also be served well chilled and is generally brought to the table in an ice bucket.

Wines to Serve with Food

Oysters, shellfish	Chablis, dry Moselle, Champagne
Fried or grilled fish	Dry Graves, Moselle, Hock, Rosé, Blanc de Blanc
Fish with sauces	Riesling, Pouilly-Fuissé, Chablis
Veal, pork or chicken dishes (served simply)	Rosé, Riesling, a light red wine such as Beaujolais
Chicken or pork served with a rich sauce	Claret, Côte de Rhône, Médoc
Rich meat dishes, steaks, game	Red Burgundy, Rioja, Red Chianti
Lamb or duck	Claret, Beaujolais
Desserts and puddings	White Bordeaux, Sauternes, Entre Deux Mers
Cheese	Burgundy, Rioja, Cabernet Sauvignon

This edition published 1992 by Wordsworth Editions Ltd, 8b East Street, Ware, Hertfordshire.

Copyright © Wordsworth Editions Ltd 1992.

Designed by Tony Selina, The Old Goat Graphic Company, London, England.

ISBN 1-85326-979-4

Printed and bound in Hong Kong by South China Printing Company.